LET'S EAT

Mexican

LET'S EAT

Mexican

Juana Maria del Campo

Editor
Wendy Hobson

foulsham
LONDON • NEW YORK • TORONTO • SYDNEY

foulsham

Bennetts Close, Cippenham, Berkshire SL1 5AP

ISBN 0-572-01729-4

Photoset in Great Britain by Typesetting Solutions, Slough, Berkshire.
Printed and bound in Great Britain by Cox & Wyman Ltd, Reading, Berkshire.

Contents

Introduction

The culinary traditions of Mexico are among the richest and most varied in the world. When the Spaniards first reached Latin America, they discovered not only a new continent, but also a wealth of foods and cooking styles hitherto unknown in Europe. The potato, the tomato, chocolate, vanilla, pineapple, turkey ... these are just a few of the foods they discovered and which are now so familiar we can scarcely imagine cooking without them. But while the ingredients have become a part of our daily diet, the huge variety of dishes which the Mexican cook creates with them are comparatively little known.

The ancient culture of the native South American Indians and the influence of their Spanish conquerors have combined to produce a cuisine that is at once simple and sophisticated. It is a cuisine that is above all suited to the family kitchen, where the aromas of its preparation will make certain that everyone is gathered in good time to relish the delights of a really fresh tortilla, or a dish of Country-Style Eggs dripping with cheese melting straight from the grill.

The history of the Mexican people is as richly varied as the land in which they live, so it is not surprising that Mexican cuisine includes a great many different ingredients and flavours. Some of the spices and dried chillies which are commonly used are not easy — or even possible — to find outside Mexico. We have therefore selected only those recipes where a tasty dish can be made using readily available ingredients.

The techniques of Mexican cookery are in some respects quite different from those which are familiar to us, but they are not complicated or difficult to master, and practising will be part of the fun! It is important to have all the ingredients ready prepared before you actually start cooking, then your family and friends can enjoy the delicious results just as the Mexicans do — straight from the oven.

The typical Mexican daily meal pattern differs from our own. It begins with *desayuno*, the first or small breakfast of coffee and a sweet roll, eaten very early in the day. This is followed later in the morning by *almuerzo*, the second or heartier breakfast, usually including fruit, an egg dish, tortillas and beans. The main meal, *comida*, is eaten in early to late afternoon. It consists of many courses including appetiser, soup, a rice or noodle dish, fish course, main course, salad, beans and dessert. This meal is generally — and understandably — followed by a siesta. In the evening, all that is wanted is a light snack, *merienda*, such as crusty rolls and sliced ham or a sweet roll and coffee. For special occasions, *cena*, a two or three course supper, is served. If you wish to try a real Mexican-style meal, there are plenty of recipes to choose from in this book.

Mexican food is full of colour, texture and wonderful spicy tastes. It is also economical and healthy. With lots of fresh vegetables and dried beans for vitamins, fibre and protein, a little meat can be stretched a long way and no one will be left feeling hungry!

When you cook Mexican-style, relax, experiment, and above all enjoy yourself, as your family and friends will undoubtedly enjoy the food you have prepared.

Ingredients

In order to give your Mexican dishes a truly authentic taste, there are two ingredients about which you should take extra care. The first of these is tomatoes and the second is chillies. If it is at all possible, you should always use the fresh versions; you will get a far better texture, colour and flavour.

All the following ingredients are common in Mexican cookery and can be bought from supermarkets and delicatessens. We have not included recipes for which the ingredients are unobtainable, but for those ingredients which are less readily available, we have suggested suitable alternatives.

Acitron
This is candied cactus, which has a pale yellow colour and a soft chewy texture. You can use candied pineapple instead.

Avocados
In Mexico there are many different varieties of avocado, which are eaten raw, as a garnish, or chopped into soup just before serving. You are unlikely to find more than a couple of varieties in the supermarket: the large, green and smooth-skinned variety, and the smaller, almost black, rough-skinned variety. It does not matter which you use, but always make sure that the fruit is quite ripe. It should give slightly if pressed gently between finger and thumb. If an avocado is hard, it will lack flavour and will not have the wonderful melting texture of the ripe fruit. Wrap a hard avocado in newspaper and put it the airing cupboard for 24 hours before use.

Avocado Leaves
If you can by any chance get hold of some avocado leaves — from a friend who has a tree, perhaps — they can be

dried and stored for use in a variety of dishes to which they impart a unique and delicate flavour. Bay leaves make a reasonable substitute, though the flavour is not the same.

Banana Leaves
Mexican cooks use banana leaves as a type of waterproof packaging for foods that must be kept dry while being cooked in boiling water. They should be warmed gently in the oven before use in order to make them pliable. Kitchen foil works just as well, but lacks the visual appeal!

Beans
Beans are a major source of protein in the Mexican diet, and also provide valuable minerals and fibre. Remember that all dried beans must be boiled continuously for at least 15 minutes in order to eliminate the toxins they contain when raw. Most beans will need a much longer cooking time before they are tender.

Cheese
Cheese presents a natural contrast of both texture and colour to the tomatoes and chillies which feature so often in Mexican food. Not surprisingly it is a widely used ingredient, and there are quite a number of regional Mexican cheeses. Unfortunately you will not find any of these in your local grocer. However, Mozzarella makes a good substitute where sliced or shredded cheese is called for; natural cream cheese — without emulsifiers — will serve very well where crumbled cheese is wanted; and a hard Cheddar will give good results in recipes requiring grated cheese. You can experiment until you get the flavour and texture you like best; perhaps trying a combination of two cheeses in order to get the flavour from one and that wonderful melting quality from another. The only cheese to be avoided is Parmesan, the strong taste of which will overwhelm the exciting blend of flavours produced by your other ingredients.

Chillies

There are many varieties of Mexican chilli, ranging from
the small, narrow, green chilli *serrano* to the waxy yellow
chilli *guero.* They are often used fresh, but they are also
dried or pickled in vinegar. You will not find individually
named varieties in your greengrocer, but it is well worth
the effort of preparing fresh chillies for most dishes rather
than using chilli powder which gives none of the texture of
the fresh fruits, and contains other spices including cumin
and garlic. Ground chilli, which is available in specialist
shops, is pure dried powdered chilli, and is used in some
dishes to achieve a completely smooth sauce.

If you have not cooked with fresh chillies before, it is
important to remember that the seeds are the hottest part.
For a spicy but still quite mild dish, leave the chillies
whole, and remove them before serving. If you like your
food a bit hotter, slice the chillies open, but discard the
seeds unless you want a really fiery result.

The juice of fresh chillies is such a strong irritant that
you must be very careful never to touch your face while
you are cutting them up, and always to wash your hands
thoroughly with soap and water when you have finished. It
is also important not to cut chillies up on a board that you
use for anything else — unless you want your apple pies to
be a lot spicier than usual!

Chorizo

These are orange or red coarse-textured sausages which
range in flavour from highly seasoned to quite hot. They
can be found in large supermarkets and delicatessens.

Lard

Where a cooking fat is needed, the Mexicans use lard in all
but the most delicate dishes. For an authentic Mexican
flavour you should do the same, and you will get the best
results if you use fresh lard from a good butcher. You can,
however, use commercial lard or substitute corn or
safflower oil and still get a delicious result. Olive oil has a

stronger and quite different flavour and should only be used where it is specified.

Masa Harina
The staple food of Mexico from the most ancient times has always been maize. This is first dried, then soaked and ground into a smooth paste called *masa*, from which corn tortillas are made. Fresh masa is not readily available, but you may be able to find *masa harina*, maize flour, which is the next best thing. It is also possible to make tortillas from ordinary wheat flour (see page 38) though the dough can be rather harder to handle. Home-made tortillas are even more delicious than ready-made ones, and since they freeze extremely well you can make a lot at a time — your trouble will be amply rewarded. Tortillas must always be served warm, so if you have made them in advance, they should be quickly reheated in a frying pan, or popped in a warm oven a few at a time, well wrapped in kitchen foil to prevent them from drying out.

Plantains
Plantains are very like bananas, but rather firmer in texture. You can find them quite easily in Indian, West Indian or other specialist greengrocers as well as some supermarkets. They are ready to use when they are black-skinned and slightly soft. Firm bananas make an excellent substitute.

Pumpkin Seeds
Health food stores and specialist grocers usually stock pumpkin seeds, but make sure they are not either toasted or salted.

Seville Oranges
These should be easy enough to find in January or February, during the marmalade-making season, and they can be frozen whole quite successfully for future use. Alternatively you can add lemon juice to ordinary orange juice to achieve the sharper taste of Sevilles.

Tomatoes Verdes or Tomatillos
These are light green fruits, about the size of a plum and with a firm texture. It is difficult to obtain them fresh but you can buy them in tins.

Tomatoes
In Mexico, tomatoes grow so abundantly that there is always a plentiful supply of fresh ones, which come in lots of different shapes and sizes. Whenever possible, you should try to use fresh tomatoes, preferably the big beefsteak or Italian plum varieties which have far more flavour. Tinned tomatoes, carefully drained, make a reasonable alternative, but if you use tomato purée the result will neither look nor taste anything like the real thing.

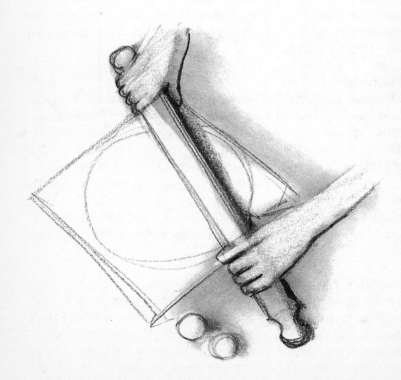

Equipment

Mexican cookery traditionally uses some specific items of kitchen equipment, but your ordinary utensils and crockery will serve equally well.

Earthenware Dishes
The Mexicans often cook and serve their food in large earthenware dishes or casseroles, called *ollas* — the original oven-to-table ware. It looks attractive and it saves washing up, but it is certainly not essential.

Food Mill
In some recipes you will achieve a more authentic, rustic result if you use an old-fashioned food mill, fitted with quite a coarse cutting disc, rather than a blender. The choice is yours, and you can experiment to see what gives the texture you prefer.

Frying Pan
A lot of Mexican dishes require a large heavy frying pan, and you will find the preparations far easier if you have two.

Griddle
If you have a griddle it will be perfect for cooking tortillas and for toasting certain ingredients before adding them to your chosen dish. However, a frying pan and a grill will make perfectly good substitutes.

Pestle and Mortar
Freshly ground herbs and spices have a far superior flavour to the ready ground alternative, and a pestle and mortar make the job of grinding them much easier. If you do use ready-ground spices, always make sure they are as fresh as possible and keep them in really airtight jars.

Cooking Methods

Skinning and Seeding Tomatoes
In order to make a smooth tomato-based sauce, the skins
must be removed, and for a really smooth result you will
need to discard the seeds as well. To do this, first plunge
the tomatoes in boiling water for a minute or so, then
remove with a slotted spoon and place them in a bowl of
cold water. You will find that it is then quite easy to cut out
the hard stem end of each tomato and slip off the skin. If
you want to remove the seeds as well, simply cut each
tomato in half and scoop out the seeds with a teaspoon.

Roasting Chillies or Green Peppers
In some recipes, the chillies or peppers are roasted, peeled,
seeded and deveined before use. To do this, put them
under a hot grill, turning occasionally, until they are
charred and blistered. Keep a close eye on this operation
since if you leave them for too long they will be burnt to a
cinder! When they are ready, put the hot chillies or
peppers in a plastic bag, seal it tightly, and leave for 15
minutes or so. It will then be quite easy to peel off the
skins under running water. Next, cut out the stem ends, slit
the chillies or peppers open and wash out the seeds and
veins. Drain on kitchen paper and don't forget to wash
your hands with soap!

Shredding Meat
This technique is quite often used in Mexican cooking and
gives a texture that is totally different from any found in
European cuisine. First cut the meat into chunks, or joint a
chicken, then put it in a pan and just cover with salted
water. Bring to the boil and then half cover with a lid so
that the meat steams, with the water kept simmering, for 45
minutes for chicken or pork to 1 hour for beef or lamb.
Remove from the heat, take off the lid, and let the meat
cool down in the broth. Drain the meat (reserving the

broth for some other dish), remove any skin and bones, then shred with a fork.

Skinning Tomatoes
To skin tomatoes, simply drop them into boiling water for about 1 minute, then place in cold water and the skins should slip off fairly easily.

Notes on the Recipes

1 Follow one set of measurements only, do not mix metric and Imperial.
2 Eggs are size 2.
3 Wash fresh produce before preparation.
4 Spoon measurements are level.
5 Adjust seasoning and strongly flavoured ingredients, such as onions and garlic, to suit your own taste.
6 If you substitute dried for fresh herbs, use only half the amount specified.

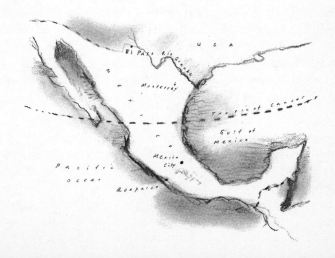

Appetisers

General Notes

The word used in Mexico for appetisers is *antojitos*. Many of the tortillas dishes that are offered as main dishes in restaurants are considered snack food in Mexico; these include tacos, tortilla turnovers or quesadillas, rolled tortillas or burritos and some other tortilla dishes. These can be adapted for use as appetisers by making them smaller — say 10 cm/4 in 'cocktail' size.

The following dishes can all be adapted in this way. Quesadillas (page 46), Beef Burritos (page 44), Tacos (page 42), Avocado Tacos (page 45), Tacos with Beans and Sausage (page 43), Stuffed Tortillas (page 52). Meat Turnovers (page 86), Meatballs (page 85), Fishballs in Tomato Sauce (page 64), Refried Beans (page 117).

1 Marinated Fish Acapulco Style

Cebiche estilo, or marinated fish, is one of the most elegant of all appetisers and is especially suitable in warm weather or before a heavy meal.

Ingredients

450 g/1 lb cod or haddock fillets, cubed
Juice of 6 limes
225 g/8 oz tomatoes, skinned, seeded and chopped
4 fresh chillies, poached in lemon juice, drained and
  chopped
60 ml/4 tbsp olive oil
15 ml/1 tbsp chopped fresh parsley or coriander
Salt and freshly ground white pepper
½ lettuce (optional)
1 red onion, thinly sliced (optional)
1 avocado, thinly sliced (optional)

Method

1. Place the fish in a bowl and pour over the lime juice. Refrigerate for 3 to 4 hours, stirring several times to make sure the fish is well marinated.

2. Add the tomatoes, chillies, oil, parsley or coriander and salt and pepper to taste and stir gently.

3. For an appetiser, serve in a dish lined with lettuce leaves and eat with small forks. For a first course, serve in small bowls or shells, garnished with slices of onion and avocado.

Serves 4

2 Guacamole

Guacamole is an avocado purée which is often served as an appetiser, but it is much more versatile in Mexican cooking. It can be used as a vegetable side dish, a salad, a sauce or a garnish; it can be an ingredient in countless dishes, and as a dip with crisp fried tortilla pieces; or an appetiser spread on hot tortillas. Placing an avocado stone in the purée is believed to keep the sauce from darkening, but to be sure of a bright green purée, make the dish as close to serving time as possible. If you have to make the dish in advance, cover it tightly with clingfilm and do not add the salt until just before serving.

Ingredients

3 *avocados, peeled*
2 *fresh chillies or chilli powder to taste*
1 *small onion, coarsely chopped*
1 *sprig of coriander*
15 *ml/1 tbsp olive oil*
Salt
30 *ml/2 tbsp freshly squeezed lemon or lime juice*

Method

1. Reserve one avocado stone if you wish, and place the avocados in a blender with the chillies or chilli powder, onions, coriander and oil. Blend to a purée, then season to taste with salt and lemon or lime juice.

2. Place in a decorative dish to serve.

Serves 4

3 Guacamole with Tomatillos

Ingredients

1 fresh chilli, seeded
1 small onion, quartered
450 g/1 lb tinned tomatillos or tomatoes, drained
3 avocados, peeled
15 ml/1 tbsp olive oil
15 ml/1 tbsp chopped, fresh coriander
Salt

Method

1. Place the chilli and onion in a small saucepan, just cover with water and simmer for about 5 minutes until tender.

2. Drain and mix with the tomatillos or tomatoes in a blender.

3. Mince the avocados or mash them with a fork, then mix in the blended ingredients with the oil, coriander, and salt to taste.

4. Place in a decorative dish to serve.

Serves 4

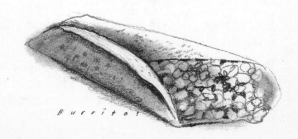

Burritos

Stuffed Cheese

This unique dish from Ucatan reflects the Dutch influence in the Caribbean.

Ingredients

1 x 2 kg/4 lb Edam cheese
3 hard-boiled eggs
450 g/1 lb ham, coarsely chopped
1 sliced white cabbage
½ onion, coarsely chopped
1 green pepper, seeded and coarsely chopped
1 tomato, skinned, seeded and chopped
250 ml/8 fl oz/1 cup water
10 green or black olives, stoned and chopped
25 g/1 oz/3 tbsp sultanas
15 ml/1 tbsp capers
Salt and freshly ground black pepper
18 Corn Tortillas (page 36)

Method

1.   Cut a 1 cm/½ in cap slice from the top of the cheese and hollow out the inside of the cheese with a spoon, leaving a 1 cm/½ in shell. Peel off the wax coating from the outside of the cheese and from the top slice. Reserve the slice, and keep the centre of the cheese for another recipe.

2.   Peel the egg whites from the eggs and chop them finely. Leave the yolks whole.

3.   Purée the ham, cabbage, onion, pepper and tomato. Place the mixture in a saucepan, add the water, bring to the boil and simmer gently for 5 minutes.

4. Add the olives, sultanas, capers and egg whites
and season to taste with salt and pepper. Stir over
a low heat until the mixture is almost dry.

5. Place half the filling into the cheese, add the egg
yolks in a layer and top with the remaining filling.
Place the cap on top of the cheese and wrap it
tightly in a muslin cloth, tying it firmly closed with
string. Set in a bowl in a steamer, cover and steam
for 15 minutes or until the shell is just soft.

6. Remove the cheese, unwrap it and discard the cap.
Place the cheese on a serving plate and serve with
hot tortillas, filled and folded like tacos.

Serves 8 to 10

Guacamole with Tomatoes

Ingredients

3 avocados, peeled and diced
450 g/1 lb tomatoes, skinned, seeded and chopped
15 ml/1 tbsp chopped onion
15 ml/1 tbsp chopped fresh coriander
15 ml/1 tbsp olive oil
1 fresh chilli, seeded and chopped
Salt

Method

1. Mix all the ingredients together thoroughly and
place in a decorative dish to serve.

Serves 4

6 Tortilla Chips

The simplest Mexican appetiser of all is freshly fried tortilla triangles, or *tostaditas*. In Mexico, they are kept warm in a basket lined with a cloth napkin and served with one or more sauces. You can use stale tortillas for this recipe. Tostaditas will keep for up to a week stored in an airtight container, so you can make several batches and just warm them through before serving.

Ingredients

8 Corn Tortillas (page 36), each cut into 6 triangles
Melted lard or corn oil to 6 mm/¼ in depth
Salt

Method

1.	Heat the lard or oil to smoking point in a heavy pan or deep fat fryer. Add the triangles in small batches, turning them until they are crisp and golden. Drain on kitchen paper and sprinkle lightly with salt.

2.	Serve warm with Tomato Sauce (page 155), Tomatillo Sauce (page 156), Guacamole (page 18) or Refried Beans (page 117).

Serves 4

Enchilada

7 Chillies with Cheese

This recipe makes a savoury and satisfying hot appetiser to spread on hot tortillas.

Ingredients

45 ml/3 tbsp olive oil
1 onion, finely chopped
4 green peppers, roasted, peeled, seeded and chopped OR
12 canned green chillies, peeled and chopped
175 g/6 oz tomatoes, skinned, seeded and chopped
250 ml/8 fl oz/1 cup double cream
225 g/8 oz Mozzarella cheese, shredded
Salt and ground white pepper

Method

1. Heat the oil in a heavy frying pan, then add the onion and cook until translucent, stirring occasionally.

2. Add the peppers and chillies and tomatoes and cook for 3 to 4 minutes until slightly thickened.

3. Stir in the cream and cook for a further 3 minutes until heated through. Add the cheese and cook just until it melts. Lightly stir in salt and pepper to taste and serve hot in a bowl over a warmer or in a chafing dish with hot tortillas.

Serves 6

8 Mexican Pizza

Ingredients

1 small red pepper, seeded and cut into strips
60 ml/4 tbsp chopped fresh coriander
3 spring onions, thinly sliced
1 fresh chilli, seeded and chopped
30 ml/2 tbsp fresh lime juice
1 clove garlic, crushed
A pinch of salt
225 g/8 oz chorizo
3 x 25 cm/10 in Wheat Flour Tortillas (page 38)
175 g/6 oz mild Cheddar cheese, shredded
175 g/6 oz Mozzarella cheese, grated

Method

1. Mix together the pepper, coriander, spring onions, chilli, lime juice, garlic and salt. Cover and leave to stand at room temperature for at least 1 hour.

2. Remove and discard the chorizo casings and crumble the sausages. Fry them in a heavy frying pan over a medium heat, for 6 minutes, stirring frequently, until browned. Drain on kitchen paper.

3. Place the tortillas on greased baking sheets and top with the chorizo. Sprinkle over the cheeses. Bake in a preheated oven at 230°C/450°F/gas mark 8 for about 10 minutes until the edges are crisp and golden and the cheese is bubbly.

4. Cut the pizzas into wedges and serve sprinkled with the pepper mixture.

Serves 4

9 Nachos

Ingredients

350 g/12 oz/2 cups Refried Beans (page 117)
1 quantity Tortilla Chips (page 22)
1 large tomato, skinned, seeded and chopped
5 ml/1 tsp chilli powder
350 g/12 oz Mozzarella cheese, shredded
350 g/12 oz mild Cheddar cheese, grated

Method

1. Reheat the beans and make the tortilla chips. Spread a little of the bean mixture on each tortilla chip. Arrange the chips in a single layer, with the edges slightly overlapping, on baking sheets. Sprinkle with tomato and chilli powder.

2. Mix together the cheeses and sprinkle over the nachos.

3. Bake in a preheated oven at 200°C/400°F/gas mark 6 for about 5 minutes until bubbling. Serve immediately.

Serves 4

Enchilada

Soups

Soups are among the glories of Mexican cooking, utilising all the favourite local ingredients.

Corn Soup

This is a lovely fresh soup, ideal for a summer day.

Ingredients

25 g/1 oz/2 tbsp butter
1 small onion, finely chopped
100 g/4 oz tomatoes, skinned, seeded and puréed
3 corn cobs
1 litre/1 ¾ pts/4 ¼ cups chicken stock
Salt and ground white pepper
60 ml/4 tbsp double cream

Method

1. Heat the butter in a small saucepan and cook the onion and tomato over a low heat until the onion is soft.

2. Scrape the kernels from the ears of corn, collecting the milky juice as you do so. Purée half the kernels, with a little chicken stock if necessary, then transfer the purée to a large saucepan with the stock, reserved corn and the onion and tomato mixture. Season to taste with salt and pepper. Bring to the boil, reduce the heat and simmer for about 15 minutes until the soup has thickened slightly.

3. Add the cream and simmer for a few minutes longer. Taste and adjust the seasoning if necessary before serving.

Serves 4

2 | Avocado Soup

Ingredients

25 g/1 oz/2 tbsp butter
15 ml/1 tbsp plain flour
1 litre/1 ¾ pt/4 ¼ cups chicken stock, hot
3 avocados, peeled
15 ml/1 tbsp finely chopped onion
45 ml/3 tbsp double cream
Salt and ground white pepper
1 Corn Tortilla (page 36)
15 ml/1 tbsp corn or safflower oil

Method

1. Heat the butter until it bubbles, then stir in the flour and cook for 2 minutes, stirring, without allowing the flour to brown.

2. Gradually stir in the stock and simmer for a few minutes until slightly thickened, stirring occasionally.

3. Meanwhile, purée the avocados, then stir in a little stock to thin the purée before pouring it into the saucepan. Add the onion and cream, season with salt and pepper and simmer for 10 minutes.

4. Meanwhile, cut the tortilla into 3 cm/1 in squares. Heat the oil to smoking point in a heavy frying pan then fry the tortilla squares until crisp and golden. Drain on kitchen paper.

5. Pour the soup into a tureen or individual bowls and sprinkle with the tortilla squares just before serving.

Serves 4

3 Lime Soup

Ingredients

60 ml/4 tbsp lard or corn or safflower oil
1 small onion, chopped
175 g/6 oz tomatoes, skinned, seeded and chopped
1 small green pepper, seeded and chopped
2 litres/3 ½ pts/8 ½ cups chicken stock
1 lime, halved
6 chicken livers, finely chopped
Salt and freshly ground black pepper
Melted lard or corn or safflower oil to 6 mm/¼ in depth
6 stale tortillas, cut into thin strips OR
4 slices stale white bread, cut into 1 cm/½ in squares

Method

1. Heat half the lard or oil and fry the onion, tomatoes and pepper until the onion is translucent.

2. Add the stock and juice of half the lime. Cut half the lime peel into strips and add it to the pan. Boil for 2 minutes, then reduce to a simmer and remove the peel.

3. Cut the remaining lime into thin slices and set aside. Heat the remaining oil to smoking point then add the livers and fry until lightly browned. Season and keep warm.

4. In another pan, heat the melted lard or oil to smoking point then fry the tortilla strips or bread squares until golden. Drain on kitchen paper.

5. Ladle the soup into individual bowls and sprinkle on the hot tortilla strips or croûtons. Serve the lime slices and chicken livers separately.

Serves 4

White Fish Soup

Ingredients

750 ml/1 ¼ pts/3 cups water
1 green pepper, roasted, peeled, seeded and minced
350 g/12 oz tomatoes, skinned and chopped
1 onion, chopped
2 cloves garlic, crushed
2.5 ml/½ tsp dried oregano
5 ml/1 tsp chopped fresh coriander
1 bay leaf
2.5 ml/½ tsp salt
450 g/1 lb white fish
2 green plums, sliced (optional)

Method

1. Bring the water to the boil in a saucepan large enough to hold the fish. Add the pepper, tomatoes, onion, garlic, oregano, coriander, bay leaf and salt and continue to boil until the onion is soft, then reduce to a simmer.

2. Lower the fish into the stock, either using a trivet or wrapping it in muslin tied at both ends with long strings. Simmer for 5 minutes, then remove it from the stock and remove the skin.

3. Return the fish to the pan, add the plums, if using, and simmer for a further 10 minutes until the plums are tender and the fish flakes when tested with a fork.

4. Remove the fish carefully, keeping it whole, remove the muslin if you have used it, and serve the fish in a deep serving dish with the soup.

Serves 4

5 Pueblan Soup

Ingredients

30 ml/2 tbsp lard or corn or safflower oil
175 g/6 oz pork loin, diced
1 small onion, finely chopped
200 g/7 oz sweet corn
2 small courgettes, diced
1 green pepper, roasted, peeled, seeded and chopped
175 g/6 oz tomatoes, skinned, seeded and puréed
1.2 litres/2 pts/5 cups chicken stock
Salt and freshly ground black pepper
1 large avocado, peeled and chopped
75 g/3 oz mild Cheddar or Mozzarella cheese, shredded

Method

1. In a flameproof casserole, heat the lard or oil to smoking point then add the pork and cook, stirring, until the meat begins to brown. Cover and cook over a low heat for 15 minutes.

2. Add the onion, corn, courgettes and pepper, mix well, then add the tomatoes and stock. Season to taste with salt and pepper. Cover and simmer gently for about 15 minutes until the vegetables are just tender.

3. Add the avocado and cheese just before serving, or serve them in separate bowls to be added to the soup at the table.

Serves 4

6 Chicken and Corn Soup

Serve this soup as a light meal with salad and tortillas or with a tortilla dish.

Ingredients

4 chicken portions
750 ml/1 ¼ pts/3 cups chicken stock
225 g/8 oz sweet corn
1 small onion, chopped
5 ml/1 tsp salt
5 ml/1 tsp lard
2.5 ml/½ tsp chilli powder
15 ml/1 tbsp masa harina
5 ml/1 tsp dark brown sugar

Method

1. Place the chicken portions in a saucepan with enough chicken stock almost to cover them. Bring to the boil, then cover and simmer gently for about 30 minutes until the chicken is cooked.

2. Add the corn, onion, salt, lard and chilli powder to taste and simmer for a further 10 minutes.

3. Mix the maize flour with a little water and stir it into the soup with the sugar until the soup thickens. Serve the soup in deep bowls.

Serves 4

7 Gazpacho

Ingredients

1.5 kg/3 lb ripe tomatoes
375 ml/13 fl oz/1 ½ cups tomato juice
1 clove garlic, crushed
30 ml/2 tbsp fresh lime juice
30 ml/2 tbsp olive oil
15 ml/1 tbsp white wine vinegar
5 ml/1 tsp salt
5 ml/1 tsp sugar
2.5 ml/½ tsp dried oregano
6 spring onions, thinly sliced
60 ml/4 tbsp finely chopped celery
½ cucumber, peeled, seeded and chopped
1 fresh chilli, seeded and chopped
1 avocado, peeled and diced
1 red pepper, seeded and chopped
30 ml/2 tbsp chopped fresh coriander
150 ml/¼ pt/⅔ cup soured cream

Method

1. Skin and finely chop 1 tomato. Purée the remaining tomatoes with the tomato juice and garlic in batches, then rub through a sieve to remove the seeds.

2. Whisk the lime juice, olive oil, wine vinegar, salt, sugar and oregano into the tomato purée. Stir in the reserved tomato with the spring onions, celery, cucumber and chilli. Cover and refrigerate for at least 4 hours, preferably 24 hours.

3. Serve the soup in chilled bowls with the avocado, pepper, coriander and cream served separately.

Serves 4 to 6

8 | Bean Soup

Ingredients

100 g/4 oz/²/₃ cup red kidney, pinto or black beans
1 litre/1 ¾ pts/4 ¼ cups water
1 small onion, halved
60 ml/4 tbsp lard
1 litre/1 ¾ pts/4 ¼ cups chicken stock
175 g/6 oz tomatoes, skinned, seeded and puréed
10 ml/2 tsp finely chopped onion
2.3 ml/½ tsp dried oregano
Salt
2 Corn Tortillas (page 36) OR slices of stale bread,
    cut into 3 cm/1 in squares
50 g/2 oz Cheddar cheese, grated

Method

1.   Wash the beans and place in a saucepan with the water and onion. Bring to the boil, add 15 ml/1 tbsp of lard and boil rapidly for 15 minutes. Cover and simmer for 1½ hours until the beans are tender.

2.   Purée the beans with a little broth until smooth, then simmer gently with the chicken stock.

3.   Heat 15 ml/1 tbsp of lard to smoking point, add the tomatoes and onion and cook over a medium heat for 5 minutes until beginning to thicken. Add to the soup with the oregano and salt.

4.   In another pan, heat the remaining lard to smoking point then fry the tortilla or bread squares until golden brown. Drain on kitchen paper.

5.   Mix the cheese into the soup, sprinkle with tortilla or bread squares and serve.

Serves 4

Tortilla Dishes

Tortillas are almost synonymous with Mexican food, and there is a whole range of dishes you can make using these delicious corn dough pancakes. It takes a little time to make your own, but you will be well rewarded.

1 Corn Tortillas

Making tortillas is an art, and patting them out by hand is an art that may require more practice than most people are willing to devote to it, though it is fun to try. Pressing tortillas is easier, much like making pastry. It does require a certain amount of experience, however, as you need to have a feel for the dough to know when it has reached for proper consistency for pressing.

The first few times you use maize flour, masa harina, it is wise to divide the dough into sections and then make one test tortilla before rolling all the sections into balls. If the dough is too wet or too dry, it can be adjusted by adding more flour or more water. If the first tortilla you press cracks as you flatten it or has crumbly edges, add a bit more water to the dough, knead it again and have another try. If you find it easier, you can make the tortillas slightly smaller.

Tortillas will keep well in the refrigerator for up to a week, or in the freezer for 6 months, sealed in a plastic bag. To reheat, wrap up to 12 tortillas in a foil parcel and heat in a moderate oven for 15 minutes.

Ingredients

275 g/10 oz/2 ½ cups masa harina
50 g/2 oz/⅓ cup plain flour
300 ml/½ pt/1 ¼ cups warm water

Method

1. Mix the flours together then stir in the water and mix to a dough, kneading as you would to make bread. Cover and leave to stand for 30 minutes.

2. Divide the dough into 12 and roll each piece into a ball. To pat the tortillas out by hand, wet your hands slightly, then pat each ball between palms and fingers, moving it gradually in a circular motion until it reaches 15 cm/6 in in diameter.

3. If you are pressing the tortillas, cut out 24 pieces of greaseproof paper about 18 cm/7 in square. Place one piece of paper on a smooth surface, place a ball of dough in the centre and cover with another sheet. Press with a flat board or flat bottom of a large saucepan until the tortilla measures about 15 cm/6 in in diameter.

4. To cook, heat a lightly greased cast iron griddle or frying pan over a medium heat. Place a tortilla on the hot griddle or pan and cook for a few minutes until the dough begins to firm, then turn it over and cook until lightly toasted; some dark spots will appear. Turn the tortilla once more and cook until lightly toasted on the second side. At this point the tortilla should puff up slightly; if it does not, adjust the heat before cooking the next tortilla.

5. Keep the tortillas warm in a basket lined with a cloth napkin while you cook the remaining tortillas.

6. If you plan to fill the tortillas, use the slightly firmer spotted side as the outside.

Makes 12 x 15 cm/6 in tortillas

2 Wheat Flour Tortillas

Wheat flour tortillas are made with a rolling pin, like pastry. They are used for burritos and make a delicious hot bread to serve spread with butter. Flour tortillas can be frozen successfully if they are separated by sheets of greaseproof paper to prevent them from sticking together. Reheat in the same way as corn tortillas.

Ingredients

450 g/1 lb/4 cups plain flour
15 ml/1 tbsp salt
75 ml/5 tbsp lard or vegetable fat
300 ml/½ pt/1 ¼ cups warm water

Method

1.   Sift together the flour and salt. Rub in the lard until the mixture resembles breadcrumbs. Stir in just enough water to form a sticky mass then turn the dough on to a floured surface and knead for about 3 minutes until smooth.

2.   Divide the dough into 20 equal balls, cover with clingfilm or a damp cloth and leave to stand at room temperature for 1 hour.

3.   Roll out each ball on a floured surface into a very thin circle about 22 cm/9 in in diameter as the tortillas will shrink slightly as they cook.

4.   Heat a lightly greased griddle or frying pan over a medium heat and cook the first tortilla until browned on the bottom, then turn and brown lightly on the other side.

5.   Keep the tortillas warm in a basket lined with a cloth napkin while you cook the remaining tortillas. Serve hot.

Makes 20 x 20 cm/8 in tortillas

3 | Dry Soup Casserole

This filling dish can be served as a main course or an
entrée along with a vegetable dish or a salad.

Ingredients

150 ml/4 fl oz/½ cup lard or corn or safflower oil
1 onion, finely chopped, 1 clove garlic, crushed
450 g/1 lb tomatoes, skinned, seeded and puréed
Salt and freshly ground black pepper
12 stale Corn Tortillas (page 36), cut into thin strips
250 ml/8 fl oz/1 cup soured cream
175 g/6 oz Mozzarella cheese, shredded
15 g/½ oz/1 tbsp butter

Method

1. Heat 15 ml/1 tbsp of lard or oil in a heavy frying
    pan and cook the onion until translucent. Add the
    garlic and tomatoes and cook for about 5 minutes
    until slightly thickened. Season to taste with salt
    and pepper. Set aside and keep warm.

2. Heat the remaining lard or oil almost to smoking
    point in another heavy frying pan and fry the
    tortilla strips lightly without allowing them to
    brown. Drain on kitchen paper.

3. Lightly butter an ovenproof casserole and layer the
    tortilla strips, tomato sauce, soured cream and
    shredded cheese, ending with a layer of cheese.
    Dot the top with butter and bake in a preheated
    oven at 180°C/350°F/gas mark 4 for about 25
    minutes until lightly browned on top.

4. As a variation, you can add 2 roasted, peeled,
    seeded and sliced green peppers with the garlic.

Serves 4

Layered Tostadas

Tostadas are open sandwiches made with tortillas rather than bread. They make a delicious appetiser served with various sauces (see page 154) or taco fillings (see page 42), or they can form the basis of a more substantial snack. Try any combination of foods you like, including hot foods and shredded lettuce, chopped tomatoes and grated cheese, or just sprinkle a tortilla with grated Mozzarella cheese, place under the grill to melt the cheese and serve with Tomato Sauce (page 155).

Ingredients

2 chicken breasts
Salt
Melted lard or corn or safflower oil to 6 mm/¼ in depth
6 Corn Tortillas (page 36)
175 g/6 oz/1 cup Refried Beans (page 117)
100 g/4 oz Mozzarella cheese, diced
90 ml/6 tbsp lard or corn or safflower oil
2 medium red potatoes, boiled in their skins and cubed
250 ml/8 fl oz/1 cup Guacamole (page 18) OR
1 avocado, peeled and thinly sliced
15 ml/1 tbsp white wine vinegar
A pinch of salt
1 onion, finely chopped
6 large lettuce leaves, shredded

Method

1. Cook the chicken breasts in a small amount of salted water in a partially covered pan for about 20 minutes until tender. Cool, then skin, bone and shred with a fork.

2   Heat the lard or oil in a heavy frying pan and fry the tortillas until almost crisp but still slightly soft in the centre. Drain on kitchen paper.

3.   Place the refried beans in a saucepan, add the cheese and heat gently until the cheese begins to melt then remove from the heat.

4.   Heat half the lard or oil in a heavy frying pan and lightly fry the potato cubes.

5.   To assemble the tostadas, spread the tortillas with a spoonful of the beans, then sprinkle on some fried potatoes and chicken, followed by guacamole or avocado slices.

6.   Mix the remaining oil with the wine vinegar and a pinch of salt. Toss the lettuce and onion in the dressing and place on top of the tostadas.

Serves 6

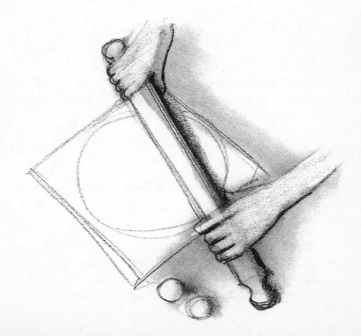

5 Tacos

Tacos are tortillas, filled and rolled and fried. The most characteristic Mexican way of cooking them is to heat them on both sides on a lightly greased griddle. To eat, they are folded into a cigar shape rather than into a half-circle.

Ingredients

Melted lard or corn or safflower oil to 6 mm/¼ in depth
8 Corn Tortillas (page 36)

Selection of fillings:
Filling for Stuffed Tortillas (page 52)
Filling for Beef Burritos (page 44)
Filling for Stuffed Peppers (page 104)
Browned Pork Bits (page 93)
Meat with Everything (page 84)
Crumbled fried chorizo sausage
Shredded cooked chicken or beef
Refried Beans (page 117)

Selection of sauces:
Tomato Sauce (page 155)
Guacamole (page 18)

Method

1. Heat melted lard or corn or safflower oil in a heavy frying pan.

2. Fill the tortillas with the chosen filling, fold and fasten closed with a cocktail stick inserted vertically. Fry the taco lightly on one side, remove the stick and fry the other side without allowing it to become crisp; it should remain pliable.

3.   Serve tacos immediately, with sauce to spoon inside. Extras such as chopped lettuce and tomatoes should be served separately.

Serves 4

 # Tacos with Beans and Sausage

Ingredients

2 chorizo sausages, skinned and chopped
45 ml/3 tbsp lard or corn or safflower oil
225 g/8 oz/1 ⅓ cups Mexican-Style Beans (page 116)
8 Corn Tortillas (page 36)

Method

1.   Fry the chorizos over medium heat until browned.

2.   In another frying pan, heat the lard or oil to smoking point and fry the beans, stirring and mashing them into a paste.

3.   Add the beans to the chorizo and cook for about 5 minutes until well heated through.

4.   Heat the tortillas on one side on a lightly greased griddle or frying pan. Place a spoonful of filling in the centre of each tortilla, roll up, heat through and serve at once.

5.   As a variation, drain the beans and cook with ½ a finely chopped onion until the onion is soft. Add 1 skinned and chopped tomato and 1 chopped chorizo. Cook until thickened and well heated. Fill hot tortillas and serve as above.

Makes 8

7 Beef Burritos

Burritos are a northern Mexican dish. Wheat flour tortillas are filled, a small portion of the top and bottom of the tortilla is folded over to hold in the filling and the tortilla is then rolled like a cigar. You can use a combination of fillings for each burrito if you like.

Ingredients

900 g/2 lb stewing beef, cubed
200 ml/7 fl oz/scant 1 cup lard or corn or safflower oil
Salt
10 ml/2 tsp chilli powder (or to taste)
4 cloves garlic
½ onion, coarsely chopped
8 Wheat Flour Tortillas (page 38)

Method

1. Pat the meat dry on kitchen paper. Heat 45 ml/3 tbsp of lard or oil to smoking point in a heavy frying pan and brown the meat in batches on all sides.

2. Place the meat in a large saucepan, add salted water to cover and bring to the boil. Reduce the heat, partially cover and simmer for about 1 ½ hours until the meat is tender. Let the meat cool in the stock, then remove it from the pan and shred with a fork.

3. While the meat is cooling, purée the chilli powder, 2 of the garlic cloves and the onion with enough water to make a smooth paste. Season to taste with salt.

4. Heat the remaining lard or oil almost to smoking point in a heavy frying pan. Crush the remaining garlic and fry until it begins to brown. Remove the garlic from the pan and fry the shredded meat, stirring continuously, until it is well browned. Stir the chilli purée into the meat and cook over a low heat until the mixture has thickened but is still moist.

5. Heat the tortillas, fill with spoonfuls of the meat mixture, then fold, roll and serve immediately.

    Makes 8

8 Avocado Tacos

Ingredients

2 avocados, peeled and mashed
5 ml/1 tsp hot made mustard
30 ml/2 tbsp double cream
15 ml/1 tbsp chopped fresh parsley or coriander
8 green or black olives, stoned and chopped
Salt and freshly ground black pepper
8 Corn Tortillas (page 36)

Method

1. Mix the avocados to a smooth paste with the mustard, cream, parsley or coriander and olives. Season to taste with salt and pepper.

2. Heat the tortillas on one side on a lightly greased griddle or in a frying pan.

3. Turn the tortillas, fill, roll, heat through and serve immediately.

    Makes 8

Quesadillas

Quesadillas are turnovers made by filling uncooked tortillas that are heated or fried. They are quick to make once you master the technique of making your own tortillas. The filled turnovers can be made in advance if they are kept tightly covered, but once they have been cooked they should be eaten immediately as they are at their best when hot and fresh. Select your favourite filling, or make a variety.

Ingredients

1 quantity Corn Tortilla dough (page 36)

Selection of fillings:
Sliced Mozzarella cheese and strips of fresh chilli
Meat with Everything (page 84)
Filling for Stuffed Tortillas (page 52)
Filling for Beef Burritos (page 44)
Browned Pork Bits (page 93)
Shredded chicken or meat with Tomato Sauce (page 155)

Method

1. Follow the recipe for tortillas, making 12 balls of dough.

2. Press or pat out the first tortilla and a place a spoonful of your chosen filling on half of each uncooked tortilla. Fold in half, pressing the edges together to close the tortilla.

3. Cook on both sides on a lightly greased griddle or in a frying pan for a few minutes until the tortilla is cooked and the filling heated through.

4.   Alternatively, heat melted lard or oil to a depth of
        6 mm/¼ in almost to smoking point and fry the
        turnovers on both sides.

Makes 12

10 Northern Burritos

Ingredients

150 g/5 oz Mozzarella cheese, sliced
8 Wheat Flour Tortillas (page 38)
1 fresh chilli, seeded and finely chopped
150 ml/¼ pt/⅔ cup Tomato Sauce (page 155) (optional)

Method

1.   Reserve a little cheese for garnish. Heat a lightly
        greased griddle or heavy frying pan over a
        medium heat. Place a tortilla on the griddle or pan,
        cover with slices of cheese and place another
        tortilla on top.

2.   When the underside of the bottom tortilla begins
        to brown and become crisp, turn the double
        tortilla over. When the bottom of the second
        tortilla has begun to brown and crisp and the
        cheese has just melted, remove from the pan.

3.   Fold the top and bottom of the tortilla over, then
        roll like a cigar and serve sprinkled with cheese
        and chilli, or with tomato sauce.

Serves 4

11 | Cheese Enchiladas

An enchilada is a tortilla that has been dipped in sauce and is then filled, rolled and eaten with a fork. Enchiladas should not be filled and then baked; they are not a casserole dish but a dish that is assembled and served quickly so that the tortillas remain intact.

Ingredients

30 ml/2 tbsp lard or corn or safflower oil
1 onion, finely chopped
1 clove garlic, crushed
450 g/1 lb tomatoes, skinned, seeded and pured
2 fresh green chillies
Salt
Melted lard or corn or safflower oil to 6 mm/¼ in depth
12 Corn Tortillas (page 36)
225 g/8 oz Mozzarella or mild Cheddar cheese, shredded

Method

1. Heat 30 ml/2 tbsp of lard or oil in a heavy frying pan, add half the onion and the garlic and cook, stirring, until the onion is translucent.

2. Add the tomato purée and chillies and cook over a medium heat for 6 to 8 minutes, stirring, until the sauce has thickened. Season to taste with salt and keep warm over a low heat.

3. Heat the lard or oil in another heavy frying pan and cook the tortillas one at a time until they are softened but not browned. Drain on kitchen paper.

4. Dip each tortilla into the warm sauce, fill with a large spoonful of cheese and the remaining onion, roll up and place in a warmed serving dish, seam side down.

5.   When all the tortillas are filled and rolled, remove
        the chillies from the sauce, pour it over the
        tortillas and serve at once.

6.   As a variation, you can substitute shredded
        chicken, beef or pork for the cheese.

        Serves 4 to 6

12 Courgette Enchiladas

Ingredients

> 2 green peppers, roasted, peeled and seeded
> 450 g/1 lb tomatoes, skinned and chopped
> 1 clove garlic
> 30 ml/2 tbsp lard or corn or safflower oil
> 15 ml/1 tbsp finely chopped onion
> 225 g/8 oz courgettes, grated
> 100 g/4 oz Mozzarella or natural cream cheese
> Melted lard or corn or safflower oil to 6 mm/¼ in depth
> 8 Corn Tortillas (page 36)

Method

1.   Purée the peppers with half the tomatoes and the
        garlic.

2.   Heat half the lard or oil and cook the tomato
        mixture over a medium heat for about 5 minutes,
        stirring continuously. Add a little water if
        necessary to make a smooth sauce.

3.   Heat the remaining lard or oil and cook the onion
        until translucent. Add the courgettes and cook
        over a medium heat, stirring, for about 10 minutes.

4. Add the remaining chopped tomatoes and cook for a further 5 minutes until the mixture is thick. Grate half the cheese. Remove the sauce from the heat and add the grated cheese.

5. Heat the lard or oil and fry each tortilla lightly without allowing them to become crisp.

6. Dip each tortilla in the tomato sauce, coating both sides, fill with a large spoonful of the courgette mixture, fold in half and place in a hot ovenproof dish. Pour over the remaining sauce.

7. Cut the remaining cheese into thin slices and place on top of the enchiladas. Bake in a preheated oven at 180°C/350°F/gas mark 4 for about 5 minutes until the cheese is just beginning to melt. Serve immediately.

Serves 4

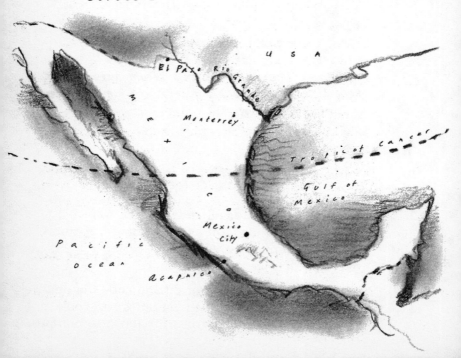

13 Swiss Enchiladas

Ingredients

4 chicken breasts
Salt
750 g/1 ½ lb tomatoes, skinned, seeded and chopped
1 small onion, quartered
1 clove garlic
120 ml/4 fl oz/½ cup corn or safflower oil
8 Corn Tortillas (page 36)
250 ml/8 fl oz/1 cup double cream

Method

1. Place the chicken in a saucepan with salted water to cover, bring to the boil, partially cover and simmer for about 30 minutes until tender.

2. Allow the chicken to cool in its broth then skin, bone and shred it with a fork.

3. Purée the tomatoes, onion and garlic. Season to taste with salt.

4. Heat 30 ml/2 tbsp of oil in a heavy frying pan and cook the tomato mixture over a medium heat for about 5 minutes, stirring, until the mixture thickens slightly. Adjust the seasoning to taste. Set aside and keep warm.

5. Heat the remaining oil in a large frying pan almost to smoking point and cook the tortillas one at a one until they are softened but not browned. Drain on kitchen paper.

6. Fill the tortillas with a spoonful of shredded chicken, roll up and place in a warmed serving dish, seam side down.

7. Pour over the tomato sauce, top with the cream and serve immediately.

Serves 4

Stuffed Tortillas

One of the seemingly infinite variations of tortilla is the *panucho,* a tortilla cooked to become hollow and then stuffed. These can be stuffed and kept tightly covered for several hours before being fried just before serving. You can use any of the taco fillings as alternatives.

Ingredients

30 ml/2 tbsp lard or corn or safflower oil
225 g/8 oz beef, finely chopped
15 ml/1 tbsp finely chopped onion
225 g/8 oz tomatoes, roasted, skinned and puréed
10 ml/2 tsp chopped fresh parsley
15 ml/1 tbsp sultanas, soaked
15 ml/1 tbsp flaked almonds
Salt
1 quantity Corn Tortilla dough (page 36)
225 g/8 oz/1 1/3 cups Refried Beans (page 117)
Melted lard or corn or safflower oil to 6 mm/¼ in depth
375 ml/13 fl oz/1 ½ cups Tomato Sauce (page 155)

Method

1. Heat the lard or oil to smoking point in a heavy frying pan and cook the meat and onion until browned.

2. Add the tomatoes and parsley and cook over a medium heat for about 10 minutes until thickened. Add the sultanas and almonds and season to taste with salt.

3. Pat or press out 12 tortillas and fry them. As each tortilla is turned for its final toasting, spotted side up, it should puff up. If not, tap it lightly with your

fingertips or press gently with a spatula to make it puff. As the tortillas cool, use a small knife to cut a slit in one edge large enough for the tortilla to be stuffed.

4. Spread a layer of beans inside each tortilla, then spread the beans with a layer of filling.

5. Heat the lard or oil in a heavy frying pan and fry the tortillas lightly. Drain on kitchen paper and serve immediately with the tomato sauce.

Makes 12

15 | Tortilla Casserole Guerrero Style

This is a quick and delicious way to use up leftover tortillas.

Ingredients

450 g/1 lb tomatoes, skinned, seeded and chopped
3 fresh chillies, seeded and chopped
50 g/2 oz/¼ cup butter
8 stale Corn Tortillas (page 36), quartered
Salt
150 ml/¼ pt/⅔ cup soured cream
100 g/4 oz Cheddar cheese, grated

Method

1. Purée the tomatoes and chillies.

2. Melt the butter in a heavy frying pan and cook the tortilla pieces until crisp but not brown. Add the tomato mixture and cook over a medium heat for about 5 minutes until the tortilla pieces begin to soften slightly. Season to taste with salt, pour over the soured cream and sprinkle with cheese and serve immediately.

Serves 4

16 | Aztec Pudding

Ingredients

4 chicken breasts
30 ml/2 tbsp lard or corn or safflower oil
1 onion, finely chopped
750 g/1 ½ lb tomatoes, skinned, seeded and puréed
Salt
4 eggs, separated
Melted lard or corn or safflower oil to 6 mm/¼ in depth
8 Corn Tortillas (page 36)
2 green peppers, roasted, peeled, seeded and cut into
    strips
350 g/12 oz mild cheese, shredded

Method

1.   Place the chicken breasts in a saucepan with salted
        water to cover, bring to the boil, partially cover
        and simmer for about 30 minutes until tender.
        Allow the chicken to cool in the broth, then skin,
        bone and shred with a fork.

2.   Heat the lard or oil in a heavy frying pan and fry
        the onion until translucent. Add the tomatoes and
        cook over a medium heat for about 5 minutes,
        stirring, until slightly thickened. Season to taste
        with salt.

3.   Beat the egg yolks lightly. Beat the egg whites until
        stiff and fold them into the yolks.

4.   Heat the 6 mm/¼ in of lard or oil to smoking
        point. Dip a tortilla into the eggs to coat both
        sides, then fry in the lard or oil until golden
        brown. Place the tortilla in a round casserole and
        sprinkle with peppers, chicken, a large spoonful of

sauce and some cheese. Continue to dip and cook the remaining tortillas and layer them in the same way, ending with a tortilla.

5. Pour any remaining egg over the top of the pudding and bake in a preheated oven at 180°C/350°F/gas mark 4 for 20 minutes until golden brown. Serve immediately.

Serves 4

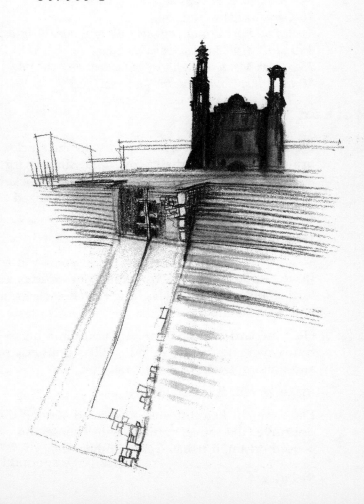

17 | Chicken Flutes

Mexican *flautas* are rolled tightly, then fried until crisp and served covered with a sauce.

Ingredients

4 chicken portions
600 ml/1 pt/2 ½ cups chicken stock
16 Corn Tortillas (page 36)
Melted lard or corn or safflower oil to 6 mm/¼ in depth
450 ml/3/4 pt/2 cups Tomatillo Sauce (page 156)
75 g/3 oz Mozzarella cheese, shredded
30 ml/2 tbsp soured cream (optional)

Method

1. Place the chicken in a saucepan with the stock, bring to the boil, partially cover and simmer for about 30 minutes until tender. Allow the chicken to cool in the stock, then skin, bone and shred with a fork.

2. Heat the tortillas briefly in a lightly greased frying pan or in foil in a moderate oven.

3. Place a spoonful of chicken along one edge of each tortilla and roll up very tightly. Fasten each tortilla with a cocktail stick.

4. Heat the lard or oil to smoking point in a heavy frying pan and fry the rolled tortillas until crisp and golden. Drain on kitchen paper.

5. Make or reheat the sauce.

6. Place the chicken flutes on a warmed serving dish, pour over the sauce, sprinkle with cheese and soured cream, if using. Serve immediately.

Serves 4

18 Little Cheese Tacos

Although called 'tacos', these are served with a sauce, like the chicken flutes.

Ingredients

2 green peppers, roasted, peeled, seeded and chopped
225 g/8 oz tomatoes, skinned, seeded and chopped
45 ml/3 tbsp lard or corn or safflower oil
30 ml/2 tbsp finely chopped onion
Salt
12 Corn Tortillas (page 36)
350 g/12 oz Mozzarella cheese
150 ml/¼ pt/⅔ cup soured cream
75 ml/5 tbsp buttermilk

Method

1. Purée the peppers and tomatoes.

2. Heat 15 ml/1 tbsp of lard or oil in a heavy frying pan and cook the onion until translucent. Add the tomato and pepper purée and cook over a medium heat, stirring, until slightly thickened. Season to taste with salt. Keep warm over a low heat.

3. Heat the remaining lard or oil in another heavy frying pan and fry the tortillas lightly until softened but not crisp. Drain on kitchen paper.

4. Cut the cheese into 12 long narrow strips. Place 1 strip on the outer edge of each tortilla and roll up tightly. Place on a warmed serving dish and cover with the sauce.

5. Mix together the soured cream and buttermilk, pour over the tortillas and serve immediately.

Makes 12

Seafood

*Mexico is abundant in seafood,
both from the sea and from fresh
water. Among the most
interesting of the many fish
dishes in the cuisine are the cold
dishes which include Three-
Coloured Fish and Fish with
Guacamole.*

1 Fish in Chilli Sauce

Ingredients

1 x 900 g/2 lb white fish fillet
120 ml/4 fl oz/½ cup olive oil
2 green peppers, roasted, peeled and seeded
1 fresh chilli, seeded
30 ml/2 tbsp lard or corn or safflower oil
3 cloves garlic, crushed
15 ml/1 tbsp finely chopped onion
5 egg yolks
450 ml/3/4 pt/2 cups water
Salt

Method

1. Brush the fish lightly with olive oil and grill for about 10 minutes, or bake in a preheated oven at 200°C/400°F/gas mark 6 for 20 minutes until the fish flakes when tested with a fork.

2. Meanwhile, purée the peppers and chilli, adding a little water, if necessary, to make a smooth purée.

3. Heat the oil in a heavy frying pan and fry the garlic until golden. Remove the garlic from the pan and add the onion and puréed peppers and chillies. Cook over a medium heat for 3 minutes, stirring, until slightly thickened. Cool slightly.

4. Beat the egg yolks with the water and mix into the chilli-onion mixture. Place over a low heat and simmer, stirring constantly without boiling, until thickened. Season to taste with salt.

5. Place the fish on a warmed serving dish and pour over the sauce. Serve immediately.

Serves 4

2 Fish with Chilli and Red Wine Sauce

Ingredients

5 ml/1 tsp chilli powder
2 cloves garlic
5 ml/1 tsp cumin seeds, ground
750 g/1 ½ lb tomatoes, skinned, seeded and chopped
1 green pepper, roasted, peeled, seeded and cut into thin strips
120 ml/4 fl oz/½ cup olive oil
250 ml/8 fl oz/1 cup red wine
2.5 ml/½ tsp dried oregano
30 ml/2 tbsp chopped fresh parsley
50 g/2 oz stoned green olives, chopped
30 ml/2 tbsp capers
Salt and freshly ground black pepper
900 g/2 lb fish fillets

Method

1. Purée the chilli powder and garlic cloves. Add the ground cumin seeds, tomatoes, pepper strips, oil, wine, oregano, parsley, olives and capers. Season to taste with salt and pepper.

2. Lightly grease an ovenproof dish and arrange layers of fish and sauce in the dish. Bake in a preheated oven at 180°C/350°F/gas mark 4 for about 30 minutes until the fish flakes easily with a fork.

Serves 4

3 Fish with Guacamole

Ingredients

30 ml/2 tbsp lard or corn or safflower oil
1 x 1.5 kg/3 lb fish
15 ml/1 tbsp olive oil
5 ml/1 tsp white wine vinegar
750 ml/1 ¼ pts/3 cups Guacamole (page 18)
50 g/2 oz/¼ cup butter
1 bunch of spring onions, trimmed to 15 cm/6 in
    lengths
12 stuffed green olives, sliced

Method

1.   Heat the lard or oil and cook the fish for about 20
      minutes on both sides, turning carefully to avoid
      breaking it. When the fish flakes easily with a fork,
      remove to a serving dish and allow to cool.

2.   Remove the skin from the body of the fish, leaving
      the head and tail intact.

3.   Mix the olive oil and wine vinegar and pour it
      over the fish. Refrigerate the fish for at least 1
      hour.

4.   Just before you are ready to serve, prepare the
      guacamole. Spread the guacamole over the fish
      and decorate the fish with the olives to resemble
      fish scales.

5.   Heat the butter in a heavy frying pan and fry the
      spring onions until just beginning to soften.
      Garnish the fish with the spring onions and serve
      immediately.

Serves 4 to 6

Three-Coloured Fish

The white, red and green colours of this dish represent the colours of the flag of Mexico. You can serve the fish hot or cold.

Ingredients

1 x 900 g/2 lb fish fillet
Salt and ground white pepper
30 ml/2 tbsp lard or corn or safflower oil
½ small onion, finely chopped
1 slice lemon
1 sprig of thyme
5 ml/1 tsp white wine vinegar
75 ml/5 tbsp water
1 slice white bread, crusts removed
30 ml/2 tbsp sesame seeds
30 ml/2 tbsp blanched almonds
30 ml/2 tbsp olive oil
1 red pepper, seeded and finely chopped
1 small bunch of watercress

Method

1. Season the fish with salt and pepper. Heat the lard or oil in a heavy frying pan and fry the fish with the onion, lemon and thyme for about 20 minutes, turning once, until the fish flakes easily with a fork. Transfer to a warmed serving dish. If you are serving the dish cold, allow the fish to cool.

2. Mix the wine vinegar and water, add the bread and leave it to soak.

3. Toast the sesame seeds lightly in a hot, ungreased frying pan, taking care not to burn them.

4.   Purée the soaked bread and liquid with the sesame
        seeds and almonds. Add the olive oil and blend to
        a smooth sauce. Pour over the fish, sprinkle with
        pepper and garnish with sprigs of watercress.

Serves 4

5 Fried Red Snapper

Ingredients

> 1 x 1.5 kg/3 lb whole red snapper
> Salt and ground white pepper
> 30 ml/2 tbsp plain flour
> 120 ml/4 fl oz/¼ cup lard or corn or safflower oil
> 1 onion, chopped
> 2 cloves garlic, crushed

Method

1.   Wash and dry the fish inside and out and dry on
        kitchen paper. Sprinkle with salt and pepper to
        taste and dust lightly with flour.

2.   Heat the lard or oil almost to smoking point in a
        large frying pan and fry the onion and garlic until
        translucent. Remove from the pan and set aside.

3.   Add the fish to the pan and fry until browned on
        the bottom, then turn carefully and cook for about
        15 minutes until the fish flakes when tested with a
        fork. Transfer to a warmed serving dish.

4.   Return the onion and garlic to the pan and warm
        it through, then spoon over the fish and serve
        immediately.

Serves 6

Fishballs in Tomato Sauce

Ingredients

For the tomato sauce:
60 ml/4 tbsp olive oil
½ onion, finely chopped
1.5 kg/3 lb tomatoes, skinned, seeded and chopped
1 sprig of parsley, chopped
1 sprig of thyme, chopped
Salt

For the fishballs:
30 ml/2 tbsp white wine vinegar
1 slice white bread, crusts removed
750 g/1½ lb cod fillets, minced
10 ml/2 tsp finely chopped onion
100 g/4 oz tomatoes, skinned, seeded and chopped
1 clove garlic, crushed
15 ml/1 tbsp chopped fresh parsley
2 eggs, beaten
1 green pepper, roasted, peeled, seeded and cut into strips
100 g/4 oz stoned black olives, chopped

Method

1. To make the tomato sauce, heat the olive oil in a heavy saucepan, add the onion and cook until golden. Add the tomatoes, parsley and thyme and cook over a medium heat, stirring, for about 10 minutes until slightly thickened. Season to taste with salt.

2. Pour the wine vinegar over the bread and leave to soak. Mix the bread with the fish, onion, tomatoes, garlic, parsley and enough egg to make a firm mixture. Form into 4 cm/1½ in balls.

3. Bring the tomato sauce to a simmer and poach the fishballs in the sauce for 20 minutes until cooked through. Transfer to a warmed serving dish.

4. Add the pepper and olives to the sauce and cook for a further 5 minutes, then pour over the fishballs and serve immediately.

Serves 4

7 | Sole in Garlic Sauce

Ingredients

6 cloves garlic, crushed
90 ml/6 tbsp olive oil
900 g/2 lb sole fillets
Juice of 2 oranges
Salt and ground white pepper
30 ml/2 tbsp chopped fresh parsley

Method

1. Mix half the garlic with half the oil. Coat the fish with this mixture and leave to marinate in a shallow ovenproof serving dish for at least 1 hour.

2. Pour half the orange juice over the fish, season to taste with salt and pepper and bake in a preheated oven at 180°C/350°F/gas mark 4 for about 20 minutes until the fish flakes easily when tested with a fork.

3. Meanwhile, heat the remaining oil in a heavy frying pan and fry the remaining garlic for 2 to 3 minutes, stirring, without allowing it to brown. Add the parsley and remaining orange juice, season to taste with salt and pepper and simmer for about 5 minutes.

4. Pour the sauce over the fish and serve immediately.

Serves 4

8 Marinated Fish Kebabs

Ingredients

2 courgettes, thickly sliced
60 ml/4 tbsp finely chopped fresh coriander
45 ml/3 tbsp fresh lime juice
1 fresh chilli, seeded and chopped
1 clove garlic, crushed
A pinch of dried oregano
Salt and freshly ground black pepper
120 ml/4 fl oz/½ cup olive oil
450 g/1 lb mackerel fillets or halibut steaks, cubed
1 green pepper, seeded and cut into chunks
4 large spring onions, thickly sliced
16 cherry tomatoes

Method

1.   Soak 8 long wooden skewers in water. Blanch the
        courgette pieces in boiling water for 2 minutes,
        then drain and rinse under cold water.

2.   Mix the coriander, lime juice, chilli, garlic and
        oregano and season to taste with salt and pepper.
        Gradually whisk in the oil. Place the fish and
        courgettes in the marinade, cover and leave to
        stand at room temperature for at least 30 minutes.

3.   Drain the fish and courgettes, reserving the
        marinade. Thread the fish, courgettes, peppers,
        spring onions and tomatoes on to the skewers and
        grill for about 10 minutes until cooked and tender,
        basting frequently with the marinade.

Serves 4

9 Baked Crab

Ingredients

2 cooked crabs
15 ml/1 tbsp lard or corn or safflower oil
1 red or green pepper, roasted, peeled and seeded and
  finely chopped
1 onion, finely chopped
350 g/12 oz tomatoes, roasted, skinned, seeded and
  puréed
45 ml/3 tbsp finely chopped green olives
30 ml/2 tbsp capers
Salt and ground white pepper
50 g/2 oz/¼ cup butter
45 ml/3 tbsp breadcrumbs
60 ml/4 tbsp olive oil

Method

1. Break off the crabs' claws and remove the meat
    from the shell, discarding the spongy material.
    Crack the claws and remove the meat. Wash the
    shells thoroughly and set aside.

2. Heat the lard or oil in a heavy frying pan and fry
    the pepper and onion until the onion is
    translucent. Add the crab meat, tomatoes, olives
    and capers and cook over a low heat, stirring, until
    slightly thickened. Season to taste with salt and
    pepper.

3. Butter the crab shells and fill with the crab
    mixture. Dust with breadcrumbs and sprinkle with
    olive oil. Bake in a preheated oven at 190°C/
    375°F/gas mark 5 for 15 minutes until lightly
    browned.

Serves 4 to 6

10 Prawns in Fiery Garlic Butter

Ingredients

750 g/1 ½ lb uncooked prawns
100 g/4 oz/½ cup butter
60 ml/4 tbsp corn or safflower oil
8 cloves garlic, finely chopped
1 fresh chilli, seeded and finely chopped
15 ml/1 tbsp fresh lime juice
A pinch of salt
6 spring onions

Method

1. Shell the prawns, if necessary, leaving the tails attached. Rinse and drain well. Spread them in an even layer in a shallow baking dish.

2. Heat the butter and oil in a heavy frying pan until the butter is foaming. Add the garlic, chilli, lime juice and salt and cook, stirring, for 1 minute. Pour the butter over the prawns.

3. Bake in a preheated oven at 200°C/400°F/gas mark 6 for about 10 minutes until the prawns are just opaque and sizzling hot. Do not overcook or the prawns will be rubbery. Garnish with spring onions and serve immediately with crusty bread.

Serves 4

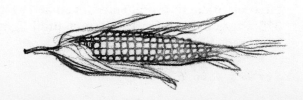

Poultry

The turkey and many other game
birds are native to Mexico, and
poultry dishes are among the
most exotic and ancient in
Mexican cuisine. The Indian
origin of many of the following
recipes can be seen in the
extensive use of seeds and nuts
as sauce ingredients.

Chicken Mexican-Style

Ingredients

60 ml/4 tbsp lard or corn or safflower oil
1 x 1.5 kg/3 lb chicken, cut into portions
1 onion, thinly sliced
2 green peppers, roasted, peeled, seeded and cut into thin
    strips
450 g/1 lb tomatoes, skinned, seeded and puréed
1 clove garlic, crushed
3 sprigs of coriander
100 g/4 oz unstoned green olives
Salt

Method

1. Heat the lard or oil almost to smoking point in a heavy frying pan and brown the chicken on all sides. Remove the chicken from the pan and fry the onion and peppers until the onion is translucent. Return the chicken to the pan with the tomatoes, garlic, 1 sprig of coriander and the olives. Season to taste with salt.

2. Cover and simmer for about 40 minutes until the chicken is tender and the sauce has thickened, adding a little water if necessary during the cooking process.

3. Adjust the seasoning to taste and serve garnished with the remaining coriander.

Serves 4

2 Chicken with Chillies

Ingredients

900 g/2 lb tomatoes, roasted, skinned and seeded
1 onion, chopped
1 clove garlic
15 ml/1 tbsp chopped fresh coriander
2.5 ml/½ tsp dried oregano
5 ml/1 tsp white wine vinegar
A pinch of ground cloves
Salt and freshly ground black pepper
1 x 1.5 kg/3 lb chicken, cut into portions
5 fresh chillies, seeded and cut into strips
75 ml/5 tbsp olive oil

Method

1. Purée the tomatoes, onion, garlic, coriander and
    oregano. Add the wine vinegar and season to
    taste with cloves, salt and pepper.

2. Place the chicken in a casserole and cover with the
    sauce and chillies. Sprinkle with the oil and bake,
    uncovered, in a preheated oven at 230°C/450°F/
    gas mark 8 for about 40 minutes until the chicken
    is tender and slightly charred and the sauce has
    been absorbed.

Serves 4

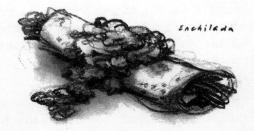

Enchilada

Chicken in Chicken-Liver Sauce

Ingredients

30 ml/2 tbsp lard or corn or safflower oil
16 chicken livers
1 clove garlic, crushed
1 onion, finely chopped
3 hardboiled egg yolks
30 ml/2 tbsp finely chopped fresh parsley
120 ml/4 fl oz/½ cup hot beef stock
Salt and freshly ground black pepper
15 ml/1 tbsp white wine vinegar
30 ml/2 tbsp olive oil
4 chicken breasts, skinned and boned
6 lettuce leaves, chopped
2 sprigs of coriander

Method

1. Heat the lard or oil in a heavy frying pan and fry the chicken livers, garlic and 15 ml/1 tbsp of the onion until the livers are browned but still slightly pink.

2. Set aside 4 of the livers. Purée the remaining livers with the egg yolks and parsley, adding enough beef stock to make a smooth sauce.

3. Pour the sauce into a saucepan, season to taste with salt and pepper and add the wine vinegar. Simmer for about 10 minutes until slightly thickened.

4. Heat the olive oil in another heavy frying pan and fry the remaining onion until translucent. Add the chicken breasts and cook over a low heat for about

30 minutes until the chicken is cooked through but not browned.

5. Pour the sauce over the chicken and cook for a further 10 minutes. Garnish with lettuce leaves and coriander and serve immediately.

Serves 4

 # Chicken in Savoury Sauce

You can use chicken or duck for this recipe.

Ingredients

175 ml/6 fl oz lard or corn or safflower oil
1 x 2 kg/4 lb chicken, cut into quarters
5 fresh chillies, seeded
100 g/4 oz/1 cup sultanas
100 g/4 oz/1 cup flaked almonds
1 slice white bread, crusts removed
120 ml/4 fl oz/½ cup white wine vinegar
½ stick cinnamon
1 clove
3 peppercorns
2.5 ml/½ tsp dried oregano
250 ml/8 fl oz/1 cup orange juice
15 ml/1 tbsp sugar
Salt

Method

1. Heat 30 ml/2 tbsp of lard or oil in a heavy flameproof casserole and brown the chicken well

on all sides. Add just enough water to prevent the meat from sticking, cover and simmer for about 45 minutes until tender.

2. Meanwhile, heat 60 ml/4 tbsp of lard or oil in a heavy frying pan and fry the chillies until soft. Remove from the pan and drain on kitchen paper. Fry the sultanas until plump, remove and drain. Fry the almonds until lightly browned, remove and drain. Fry the bread until lightly browned, remove and drain. Purée all these ingredients, adding the wine vinegar to make a smooth sauce.

3. Grind the cinnamon, clove, peppercorns and oregano together and add to the chilli mixture.

4. Heat the remaining lard or oil in the same frying pan and cook the sauce over a high heat for 5 minutes, stirring continuously. Add the orange juice and sugar and season to taste with salt.

5. Use a slotted spoon to transfer the chicken to the sauce, partially cover and simmer for 20 minutes before serving.

Serves 4

5 Chicken with Onions

This recipe appears to include an enormous amount of nutmeg, but the long slow cooking process blends all the flavours together to make a rich, savoury sauce. New peas cooked in butter are a good choice for an accompanying vegetable. This dish is also very good reheated.

Ingredients

60 ml/4 tbsp lard or corn or safflower oil
1 x 1.5 kg/3 lb chicken, cut into portions
3 large onions, chopped
1 clove garlic
600 ml/1 pt/2 ½ cups water
5 ml/1 tsp dried thyme
1 bay leaf
3 sprigs of coriander
Salt and freshly ground black pepper
1 whole nutmeg

Method

1. Heat the lard or oil almost to smoking point in a heavy flameproof casserole and brown the chicken on all sides. Remove the chicken from the pan and fry the onions and garlic over a low heat for about 20 minutes, stirring, until deep golden brown.

2. Return the chicken to the pan with the water, thyme, bay leaf and 1 sprig of coriander. Season to taste with salt and pepper. Grate the nutmeg over the chicken, cover and simmer for about 1½ hours until the chicken is very tender and the sauce is dark and thick.

3. Serve garnished with the remaining coriander.

Serves 4

6 Tablecloth Stainer Chicken

This is a very traditional Mexican dish with an exuberant combination of chicken and pork, vegetables and fruit in a red chilli sauce that gives the stew its name.

Ingredients

1 kg/2 ¼ lb chicken portions
225 g/8 oz pork spareribs, cut into serving pieces
1 small sweet potato or yam
Salt
45 ml/3 tbsp lard or corn or safflower oil
½ slice white bread, crusts removed
5 ml/1 tsp chilli powder
1 clove garlic
1 small onion, chopped
10 ml/2 tsp chopped peanuts
350 g/12 oz tomatoes, skinned, seeded and chopped
10 ml/2 tsp sugar
10 ml/2 tsp white wine vinegar
100 g/4 oz shelled peas
2 apples, peeled, cored and sliced
1 slice fresh pineapple, cut into chunks
1 ripe plantain or firm banana, diagonally sliced

Method

1.   Place the chicken, pork and sweet potato or yam in separate saucepans with salted water to cover. Bring to the boil, partially cover and simmer until tender. This will take about 45 minutes for the chicken and pork and 20 minutes for the sweet potato or yam. Allow the chicken and pork to cool in their stock, then drain, reserving 300 ml/½ pt/

1¼ cups of each of the stocks. Drain the sweet potatoes or yams, peel them and cut them into thick slices.

2. Heat 15 ml/1 tbsp of lard or oil almost to smoking point in a heavy frying pan and fry the bread until golden. Purée the bread with the chilli, garlic, onion, peanuts and tomatoes, adding a little meat stock to make a smooth purée.

3. Heat the remaining oil in a heavy frying pan and cook the purée over a medium heat for 3 minutes, then add the reserved stocks and simmer for about 10 minutes. Stir in the sugar and wine vinegar and season to taste with salt.

4. Place the chicken and pork in a large flameproof casserole and add the chilli sauce. Add the peas, apples, sweet potatoes or yams and pineapple. Simmer for a further 10 minutes and adjust the seasoning to taste. Add the plantain or banana, heat through for a few minutes and serve in deep bowls.

Serves 4 to 6

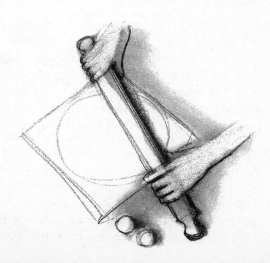

7 | Chicken in Red Wine

Ingredients

120 ml/4 fl oz/½ cup olive oil
120 ml/4 fl oz/½ cup white wine vinegar
1 onion, sliced
2 cloves garlic, crushed
1 bay leaf
1 sprig of thyme, chopped
Salt and freshly ground black pepper
2 x 1.25 kg/2 ½ lb chickens, cut into portions
4 rashers bacon, cut into squares
750 g/1 ½ lb tomatoes, skinned, seeded and chopped
2 carrots, chopped
6 spring onions, cut into 3 cm/1 in pieces
450 ml/3/4 pt/2 cups dry red wine

Method

1. Combine the oil, wine vinegar, onion, garlic, bay leaf, thyme, salt and pepper. Add the chicken and marinate for 24 hours.

2. Lightly fry the bacon in a heavy frying pan until all the fat has been rendered out. Add the tomatoes, carrots and spring onions and cook over a medium heat for 5 minutes. Add the chicken and marinade. Add the wine and bring to the boil. Cover and simmer for about 1 hour until the chicken is tender. Remove the bay leaf and serve.

Serves 6

8 | Almond Chicken

Ingredients

4 chicken breasts, boned and skinned
100 g/4 oz/1 cup ground almonds
30 ml/2 tbsp corn or safflower oil
15 ml/1 tbsp butter
1 small onion, finely chopped
1 fresh chilli, roasted, seeded and finely chopped
1 tomato, skinned, seeded and chopped
1 clove garlic, crushed
120 ml/4 fl oz/½ cup chicken stock
A pinch of salt
120 ml/4 fl oz/½ cup whipping cream
1 tomato, cut into wedges
1 sprig of coriander

Method

1. Coat the chicken in the almonds.

2. Heat half the oil and the butter. Add the chicken and cook for about 6 minutes until light brown on both sides, reducing the heat if necessary. Remove from the pan.

3. Add the remaining oil to the pan with the onion, chilli, chopped tomato and garlic and fry for 1 minute. Add the stock, salt and remaining almonds and bring to the boil.

4. Return the chicken to the pan and reduce to a low heat. Cover and simmer for 20 minutes until cooked. Transfer the chicken to a warmed serving dish.

5. Add the cream, bring back to the boil and cook, stirring, until the sauce is thickened then pour over the chicken and garnish with tomato and coriander.

Serves 4

Turkey in Red Sesame Sauce

You can use pork spareribs or chicken portions instead of turkey for this recipe if you prefer.

Ingredients

3 fresh chillies
90 ml/6 tbsp lard or corn or safflower oil
450 g/1 lb tomatoes, roasted and skinned
1 onion, chopped
1 clove garlic, toasted
l.5 kg/3 lb turkey portions
1 litre/1 3/4 pts/4 ¼ cups chicken stock
175 g/6 oz sesame seeds
8 cloves
½ stick cinnamon
Salt

Method

1.   Cut open the chillies and remove the seeds and veins. Reserve 15 ml/1 tbsp of the seeds (or to taste). Heat 30 ml/2 tbsp of lard or oil in a heavy frying pan and fry the chillies lightly. Purée the chillies with the tomatoes, onion and garlic.

2.   Place the turkey and stock in a large saucepan, bring to the boil, partially cover and simmer for about 45 minutes until the turkey is tender. Leave the turkey to cool in the stock, then drain and reserve the stock.

3.   Toast the sesame seeds and reserved chilli seeds very lightly in a hot, ungreased frying pan, stirring constantly and taking care not to burn them. Grind the seeds with the cloves and cinnamon stick.

4. Heat the remaining lard or oil and fry the ground seeds lightly, stirring constantly, until the mixture begins to form a mass. Add the tomato purée mixture and fry over a medium heat for 4 minutes. Add the reserved stock and boil the sauce until it has thickened slightly.

5. Add the turkey and ground spices and season to taste with salt. Cook over a low heat for about 15 minutes until the turkey is heated through.

Serves 4

10 Cold Spiced Duck

Ingredients

2 ducks
Salt and ground white pepper
25 g/1 oz bacon, cut into strips
2 cloves garlic, crushed
1 bay leaf
A pinch of ground cloves
A pinch of ground cinnamon
A pinch of ground nutmeg
250 ml/8 fl oz/1 cup chicken stock
120 ml/4 fl oz/½ cup dry white wine
1 Seville orange, peeled and cut into segments
1 onion, cut into wedges
A pinch of dried thyme
Green or black olives and capers

Method

1.   Sprinkle the ducks inside and out with salt and pepper and stuff with the bacon, garlic and bay leaf. Sprinkle the outside with spices and wrap tightly in muslin.

2.   Place the birds and stock in a large saucepan and cover tightly. Simmer for about 1 hour until tender.

3.   Unwrap the birds, then return to the pan with the wine, orange, onion and thyme and salt and pepper. Cover and cook over a low heat for a 10 minutes until the onions are partly cooked.

4.   Remove from the heat, take off the lid and leave the duck to cool to room temperature, then remove from the pot, cut into serving pieces and place on a serving dish. Garnish with olives and capers and pass the sauce separately.

Serves 4

Meat

*The Spanish brought many meat
dishes to Mexico and these were
soon assimilated into the
country's cuisine, cooked with
sauces made of chillies, tomatoes,
nuts and seeds and used in
tortilla dishes.*

Meat with Everything

Ingredients

750 g/1 ½ lb stewing steak, cubed
175 g/6 oz tomatoes, skinned, seeded and chopped
1 small onion, chopped
1 clove garlic, crushed
1 fresh chilli, seeded and finely chopped
40 g/1 ½ oz lard
90 ml/6 tbsp white wine vinegar
10 ml/2 tsp capers
30 ml/2 tbsp chopped green olives
3 peppercorns, crushed
1/3 stick cinnamon, ground
A pinch of ground cloves
75 g/3 oz/½ cup flaked almonds
1 bay leaf
A pinch of dried thyme
A pinch of dried marjoram
A pinch of dried oregano
Salt
8 Corn Tortillas (page 36)

Method

1. Place the beef in a large saucepan and add enough
    water to half cover the meat. Add all the
    remaining ingredients except the salt, bring to the
    boil and simmer, uncovered, for at least 1 hour
    until the liquid has evaporated and the meat is
    tender but not falling apart.

2. Season to taste with salt and serve wrapped in hot
    tortillas.

Serves 4

2 | Meatballs

Ingredients

450 g/1 lb tomatoes, skinned and seeded
5 ml/1 tsp chilli powder
15 ml/1 tbsp lard or corn or safflower oil
15 ml/1 tbsp finely chopped onion
1 clove garlic, crushed
250 ml/8 fl oz/1 cup beef stock or water
Salt
350 g/12 oz best minced beef
350 g/12 oz minced pork
25 g/1 oz/2 tbsp breadcrumbs
45 ml/3 tbsp milk
2.5 ml/½ tsp dried thyme
15 ml/1 tbsp chopped fresh parsley
1 egg, beaten
1 jar stoned olives (optional)

Method

1. Purée the tomatoes and chilli powder.

2. Heat the lard or oil and fry the onion and garlic until the onion is translucent. Add the tomato purée and cook over a medium heat for 4 minutes. Add enough stock or water to make a thin sauce and season to taste with salt. Keep over a low heat.

3. Mix the minced meats. Soak the breadcrumbs in the milk until soft, then stir into the meat. Add the herbs and enough egg to make a stiff consistency.

4. Form the mixture into balls, tucking an olive into the centre of each, if using. Drop the meatballs into the simmering sauce, cover and simmer for about 30 minutes until cooked through.

Serves 4

3   Meat Turnovers

Ingredients

450 g/1 lb minced beef
2 potatoes, cooked, peeled and cubed
100 g/4 oz cooked peas
15 ml/1 tbsp finely chopped onion
100 g/4 oz sultanas
A pinch of ground cinnamon
A pinch of ground cloves
Salt and freshly ground black pepper
120 ml/4 fl oz/½ cup Madeira or sweet sherry
225 g/8 oz/2 cups plain flour
5 ml/1 tsp baking powder
2.5 ml/½ tsp salt
30 ml/2 tbsp lard
120 ml/4 fl oz/½ cup iced water
Melted lard or corn or safflower oil to 6 mm/¼ in depth
15 ml/1 tbsp caster sugar (optional)

Method

1.   Fry the meat in a heavy frying pan until browned, then drain off the fat. Stir in the potatoes, peas, onion and sultanas. Add the spices and season to taste with salt and pepper. Add the Madeira or sherry and simmer over a medium heat for 5 minutes until the wine is reduced and the meat mixture is almost dry.

2.   To make the pastry, sift together the flour, baking powder and salt. Rub the lard into the dry ingredients until the mixture resembles fine breadcrumbs, then add enough iced water to form a smooth dough.

3.   Roll out the dough on a floured board and cut 12 circles about 10 cm/4 in in diameter.

4. Put a spoonful of filling on one half of each circle, wet the edges with water, fold over and press the edges firmly together with a fork. Leave the turnovers to dry for 1 hour.

5. Heat the lard or oil in a heavy frying pan and fry the turnovers until browned on both sides. Drain on kitchen paper and sprinkle lightly with sugar, if using, while they are still hot.

Makes 12

Pot Roast with Vegetables

Ingredients

30 ml/2 tbsp lard or corn or safflower oil
1.5 kg/3 lb beef roasting joint
2 large onions, sliced
3 cloves garlic, crushed
750 ml/13 fl oz/3 cups beef stock
1 fresh chilli, seeded and finely chopped
2.5 ml/½ tsp dried thyme
2.5 ml/½ tsp dried oregano
350 g/12 oz canned tomatillos, drained
2 courgettes, diced
12 small new potatoes
60 ml/4 tbsp finely chopped fresh coriander

Method

1. Heat the lard or oil in a large flameproof casserole and brown the beef on all sides. Remove from the pan.

2. Add the onions and garlic and fry over a medium heat for about 8 minutes until soft. Add the stock, chilli, thyme and oregano and bring to the boil. Add the tomatillos and return the beef to the pan, pushing it down so that it is surrounded by liquid. Partially cover and simmer for 2½ hours.

3. Add the courgettes and potatoes to the pan, cover and simmer for a further 40 minutes until the beef is cooked and the vegetables tender.

4. Transfer the beef and vegetables to a warmed serving plate and keep warm. Purée half the cooking sauce until smooth then return it to the

pan and cook over a medium heat for about 25
minutes, stirring occasionally, until reduced to 1
litre/1 ¾ pts/4 ¼ cups. Stir in the coriander.

5. Serve the beef cut across the grain into thin slices
with the sauce served separately.

Serves 6 to 8

5 | Pork Tamale

These are traditionally made with banana leaves and
look wonderful if you can find them, but kitchen foil is
equally effective.

Ingredients

450 g/1 lb pork shoulder, cubed
750 ml/1 ¼ pts/3 cups water
1 onion
2 cloves garlic
350 g/12 oz canned tomatillos, drained
3 fresh chillies, roasted, peeled and seeded
175 g/6 oz/3/4 cup lard
225 g/8 oz/2 cups masa harina
7.5 ml/1 ½ tsp salt
7.5 ml/1 ½ tsp baking powder
8 small lettuce leaves, halved
2 tomatoes, cut into wedges

Method

1. Place the pork, water, half the onion and 1 clove of
garlic in a saucepan and bring to the boil. Partially
cover and simmer for about 30 minutes until the
pork is tender. Drain the pork, reserving 375 ml/
13 fl oz/1 ½ cups of stock.

2.   Purée the remaining onion and garlic with the tomatillos and chillies until smooth.

3.   Heat 30 ml/2 tbsp lard in a heavy frying pan and add the tomatillo mixture. Cook for about 4 minutes, stirring, until slightly thickened. Stir in the pork and simmer for about 20 minutes, stirring occasionally, until the pork is tender.

4.   Mix the masa harina, salt and baking powder. Beat the remaining lard until light and fluffy, then beat in the masa mixture a little at a time until thoroughly blended. Heat the reserved pork stock and gradually beat it into the masa mixture to form a soft moist dough.

5.   Cut 16 x 20 cm/8 in squares from kitchen foil. Spread about 30 ml/2 tbsp of dough into an 8 cm/ 3 in square on the centre of each piece of foil. Top with about 30 ml/2 tbsp of pork mixture and cover with half a lettuce leaf. Fold the sides then the ends of the foil over the filling to enclose.

6.   Line a steamer basket with a piece of foil and arrange the tamales, seam side down, on the foil. Place the steamer basket over a pan of boiling water and cover. Simmer gently for about 1 hour until the dough is cooked. Transfer to a warmed serving dish and serve garnished with tomatoes.

Serves 4

6 | Pork Loin in Orange Sauce

Ingredients

1 kg/2 ¼ lb boneless pork loin
10 ml/2 tsp ground cinnamon
A pinch of ground cloves
Salt and freshly ground black pepper
30 ml/2 tbsp corn or safflower oil
1 small onion, chopped
1 clove garlic
175 ml/6 fl oz/¾ cup orange juice
175 ml/6 fl oz/¾ cup hot water
50 g/2 oz/⅓ cup sultanas
15 ml/1 tbsp capers
25 g/1 oz/¼ cup flaked almonds
1 large orange, peeled, sliced and seeded

Method

1. Sprinkle the pork with the cinnamon, cloves and salt and pepper. Heat the oil and brown the meat on all sides, adding the onion and garlic towards the end of cooking time.

2. When the onion is tender, pour in the orange juice and water. Cover and cook over a low heat for about 1½ hours until the meat is tender, adding a little more orange juice and water during cooking if necessary.

3. When the meat is tender, remove it from the pan with the garlic. Add more orange juice and water, if necessary, to make about 200 ml/7 fl oz/scant 1 cup of liquid. Add the sultanas and capers, bring to the boil and boil to reduce the liquid slightly. Just before serving, add the almonds.

4. Serve the meat with the sauce and garnish with the orange slices.

Serves 4

7 Tangy Braised Lamb

Refried Beans (page 117) make a good accompaniment to this dish.

Ingredients

30 ml/2 tbsp lard or corn or safflower oil
4 large lamb chump chops
2 onions, sliced
2 cloves garlic, crushed
1 fresh chilli, seeded and chopped
5 ml/1 tsp dried oregano
2.5 ml/½ tsp ground cumin
350 g/12 oz canned tomatillos, drained
250 ml/8 fl oz/1 cup beef stock
1 bay leaf
15 ml/1 tbsp cider vinegar
½ lettuce, shredded
Stoned green or black olives

Method

1. Heat half the oil and brown the meat on all sides. Remove from the pan.

2. Add the remaining oil and fry the onions, garlic and chilli until soft. Stir in the oregano, cumin and tomatillos and cook for 2 minutes, stirring constantly.

3. Add the stock and bay leaf to the pan and bring to the boil. Add the lamb, cover and simmer over a low heat for about 1 hour until the lamb is tender.

4. Transfer the lamb to a warmed serving dish and keep warm. Skim and discard the fat from the cooking sauce and stir in the cider vinegar. Boil

the sauce for about 10 minutes until thickened, spoon over the lamb and serve garnished with lettuce and olives.

Serves 4

8 Browned Pork Bits

Ingredients

1 kg/2 ¼ lb pork shoulder, cubed
1 small onion, chopped
Salt and freshly ground black pepper
8 Corn Tortillas (page 36)

Method

1. Place the meat in a flameproof casserole with enough salted water to half cover the meat. Add the onion and season to taste with salt and pepper. Bring to the boil and simmer, uncovered, for up to 2 hours until all the liquid has evaporated and the pork bits have browned in their own fat.

2. If the liquid evaporates before the meat is tender, add a little more water. Adjust the seasoning to taste and serve wrapped in hot tortillas.

Serves 4

9 Mexican Rabbit Pie

Ingredients

For the filling:
25 g/1 oz/2 tbsp butter
30 ml/2 tbsp corn or safflower oil
1 rabbit, cut into portions
2 onions, sliced
1 sprig of thyme
1 sprig of marjoram
100 g/4 oz bacon, chopped
2 large leeks, chopped
750 g/1 ½ lb tomatoes, skinned seeded and puréed
2.5 ml/½ tsp dried oregano
50 g/2 oz chopped stoned green olives
30 ml/2 tbsp capers
Salt

For the pastry:
4 eggs, separated
350 g/12 oz/3 cups plain flour
5 ml/1 tsp baking powder
2.5 ml/½ tsp salt
175 g/6 oz/¾ cup butter

1 egg yolk
15 ml/1 tbsp water

Method

1.   To make the filling, heat the butter and oil in a
        flameproof casserole and brown the rabbit lightly
        on all sides. Add one onion and cook until tender.
        Add the thyme and marjoram and enough water
        to cover the rabbit, bring to the boil, cover and
        simmer for about 1 hour until the rabbit is tender.
        Allow the rabbit to cool in the stock.

2.   Remove the rabbit from the pan, reserving the stock. Remove the meat from the bones and chop roughly.

3.   Fry the bacon in a heavy frying pan until the fat is rendered out. Chop the remaining onion, add this to the pan with the leeks and fry until the onion is translucent. Add the tomatoes and cook for 4 minutes until slightly thickened. Add about 120 ml/4 fl oz/½ cup of reserved rabbit stock, the chopped rabbit, oregano, olives and capers to make a thick sauce. Simmer for about 10 minutes and season to taste with salt.

4.   To make the pastry, beat the egg whites until stiff. Sift the dry ingredients together. Cream the butter, then add the egg yolks one at a time, mixing well. Stir the butter and egg mixture into the dry ingredients, then fold in the egg whites and form into a smooth dough.

5.   Divide the dough in half and roll out into two circles on a floured board. Place one circle inside a buttered earthenware dish, fill with the filling and cover with the second pastry circle, damping and sealing the edges and making 2 or 3 slashes in the top. Mix the egg yolk and water and use the mixture to glaze the pie.

6.   Bake in a preheated oven at 180°C/350°F/gas mark 4 for about 30 minutes until the crust is golden brown. Cool slightly before serving, or serve at room temperature.

Serves 4 to 6

10 | Veal in Walnut Sauce

Ingredients

1.5 kg/3 lb veal shoulder or breast
2 onions
1.5 litres/2 ½ pts/6 cups water
4 cloves garlic
1 sprig of thyme
5 ml/1 tsp salt
25 g/1 oz/2 tbsp butter
275 g/10 oz/1 ¼ cups ground walnuts
375 ml/13 fl oz/1 ½ cups double cream
Salt and ground white pepper
25 g/1 oz/¼ cup toasted chopped almonds

Method

1. Place the veal in a large saucepan with 1 onion, cut into quarters. Add the water, garlic, thyme and salt. Bring to the boil, skim, then cover and simmer for about 1 hour until tender.

2. Allow the meat to cool in its stock, then remove from the pan, strain and reserve the stock. Cut the meat into thin strips and set aside.

3. Mince the second onion. Heat the butter in a heavy frying pan and fry the onion until golden. Add the walnuts, cream and reserved veal stock and season to taste with salt and pepper. Bring to a simmer, add the veal and simmer until the sauce is slightly thickened. Serve sprinkled with almonds.

Serves 4 to 6

Egg Dishes

*Mexican egg dishes are perfect for
light lunches or suppers. Most of
them are spicy combinations of
egg, tomatoes and chillies, best
served hot with fresh tortillas and
fresh fruit.*

Scrambled Eggs with Tomato Sauce

Ingredients

30 ml/2 tbsp lard or corn or safflower oil
2 green peppers, roasted, peeled, seeded and cut into strips
1 clove garlic, crushed
15 ml/1 tbsp finely chopped onion
450 g/1 lb tomatoes, skinned, seeded and chopped
30 ml/2 tbsp water
1 fresh chilli, chopped (optional)
Salt and freshly ground black pepper
6 eggs, beaten
100 g/4 oz Mozzarella cheese, grated

Method

1.   Heat the lard or oil in a heavy frying pan and fry the peppers, garlic and onion until the onion is translucent.

2.   Add the tomatoes, water and chilli, if using, and cook over a medium heat, stirring, until the sauce has thickened slightly. Season to taste with salt and pepper.

3.   Lower the heat, add the beaten eggs and cook, stirring until the eggs are just set.

4.   Add the cheese and cook for a few seconds until the cheese begins to melt. Transfer to a warmed serving dish and serve immediately.

Serves 4

2 | Country-Style Eggs

Ingredients

120 ml/4 fl oz/½ cup lard or corn or safflower oil
1 onion, chopped
1 clove garlic, crushed
350 g/12 oz tomatoes, skinned, seeded and puréed
1 fresh chilli, seeded and minced
Salt
8 eggs
4 Corn Tortillas (page 36)
100 g/4 oz Mozzarella cheese, sliced
2 avocados, peeled and sliced (optional)

Method

1. Heat 15 ml/1 tbsp of lard or oil and cook the onion and garlic until translucent.

2. Add the tomato purée and chilli and simmer for a few minutes until the sauce thickens slightly. Season with salt and keep warm over a low heat.

3. In another frying pan, heat half the remaining lard or oil and fry the eggs over a low heat until the white is almost opaque, baste with the hot oil. Carefully transfer the eggs to a plate and keep them warm.

4. Add the remaining lard or oil to the pan and heat almost to smoking point then cook the tortillas until soft but not brown. Drain on kitchen paper.

5. Place tortillas on individual plates, top with 2 fried eggs, spoon the sauce over the eggs and top with slices of cheese. Place under a grill until the cheese is beginning to melt, then garnish with avocado slices, if using, and serve immediately.

Serves 4

3 Scrambled Eggs with Vegetables and Ham

Ingredients

225 g/8 oz shelled peas
45 ml/3 tbsp lard or corn or safflower oil
100 g/4 oz ham, diced
4 small courgettes, diced
3 medium potatoes, boiled, peeled and diced
1 red or green pepper, finely chopped
15 ml/1 tbsp finely chopped onion
15 ml/1 tbsp chopped fresh parsley
6 eggs, beaten
Salt and freshly ground black pepper

Method

1. Cook the peas in boiling salted water for 10 minutes until almost tender. Drain, rinse under cold running water and set aside.

2. Heat the lard or oil in a heavy frying pan and fry the ham until lightly browned. Remove with a slotted spoon.

3. In the same pan, fry the courgettes for 2 minutes, stirring, then cover and cook over a low heat for 5 minutes until almost tender.

4. Add the potatoes and pepper and cook for 2 or 3 minutes, stirring carefully to avoid breaking up the potatoes.

5. Add the onion and parsley and continue to cook until the onion is translucent.

6. Add the eggs, peas and ham and sprinkle with salt. Stir constantly until the eggs are just beginning to set. Sprinkle with pepper and serve immediately.

Serves 4

4 Shredded Beef with Eggs

Ingredients

1 kg/2 ¼ lb stewing beef, cubed
90 ml/6 tbsp lard or corn or safflower oil
1 small onion, finely chopped
3 fresh chillies, seeded and finely chopped
450 g/1 lb tomatoes, skinned, seeded and chopped
Salt
3 eggs, beaten

Method

1. Place the beef in a large saucepan with salted water to cover. Bring to the boil then reduce the heat, cover and simmer for about 45 minutes until the meat is tender. Cool the meat slightly in the stock, then drain and shred with a fork.

2. Heat 30 ml/2 tbsp of lard or oil in a large frying pan and cook the onion until translucent. Add the chillies and tomatoes and cook over a medium heat for 3 minutes. Season to taste with salt.

3. In another large frying pan, heat the remaining lard or oil almost to smoking point, add the shredded beef and cook, stirring, until lightly browned. Add the tomato mixture and simmer for 3 minutes then stir in the eggs and cook until they are just set. Serve immediately.

Serves 4

Mexican Potato Omlette

Ingredients

8 eggs
30 ml/2 tbsp cold water
Salt and freshly ground black pepper
30 ml/2 tbsp lard or corn or safflower oil
1 large potato, diced
6 spring onions, finely chopped
½ red or green pepper, seeded and finely chopped
1 fresh chilli, seeded and finely chopped
30 ml/2 tbsp finely chopped fresh coriander
1 tomato, cut into wedges

Method

1. Lightly whisk the eggs and water and season to taste with salt and pepper.

2. Heat the lard or oil in a nonstick frying pan and add the potato, onion and pepper for about 6 minutes until the potato is tender. Stir in the chilli.

3. Pour in the egg mixture and cook over a medium heat, stirring with the back of a fork for about 2 minutes until the bottom starts to set. Lift up the edges and let the uncooked mixture run to the bottom. Cook for about 2 minutes without stirring until the bottom is golden and the top is set.

4. Sprinkle the omelette with cheese and coriander, cut into wedges and serve immediately garnished with tomato.

Serves 4

Vegetables

*The number of vegetables native
to Latin America is amazingly
large. Vegetables have become an
integral part of the Mexican
cuisine, and many vegetable
dishes can be used as main
courses, such as Stuffed Peppers,
Peppers in Walnut Sauce, Stuffed
Avocados and Courgettes with
Corn.*

1 Stuffed Peppers

Ingredients

For the filling:
350 g/12 oz pork shoulder, cubed
350 g/12 oz veal shoulder or breast, cubed
30 ml/2 tbsp lard or corn or safflower oil
1 small onion, finely chopped
225 g/8 oz tomatoes, roasted
30 ml/2 tbsp flaked almonds
30 ml/2 tbsp pine kernels
30 ml/2 tbsp chopped acitron or candied pineapple
15 ml/1 tbsp white wine vinegar
A pinch of ground cinnamon
Salt and freshly ground black pepper
A pinch of sugar

For the sauce:
450 g/1 lb tomatoes, roasted
1 small onion, finely chopped
½ stick cinnamon
Salt and freshly ground black pepper

8 green peppers, roasted and peeled
3 eggs, separated
150 ml/¼ pt/⅔ cup lard or corn or safflower oil
25 g/1 oz/¼ cup flour
15 ml/1 tbsp finely chopped parsley

Method

1.   To make the filling, place the meats in a large
        saucepan and just cover with salted water. Bring to
        the boil, partially cover and simmer for about 45
        minutes until the meat is tender.

2.   Allow the meat to cool in the broth, then remove
        and shred the meat. Strain the broth and skim off

as much fat as possible. Reserve 15 ml/1 tbsp of fat and 300 ml/½ pt/1¼ cups of broth.

3. Heat the lard or oil in a heavy frying pan and fry the meat and onion until lightly browned. Add the tomatoes and cook over a medium heat, stirring, for about 5 minutes until slightly thickened.

4. Add the remaining filling ingredients and cook for a further 3 minutes. Adjust the seasoning to taste.

5. To make the sauce, purée the tomatoes and onion. Heat the reserved fat in a medium saucepan, add the tomato mixture and cook over a medium heat, stirring, for 3 minutes. Add the reserved stock, bring to the boil and add the cinnamon and season to taste with salt and pepper. Simmer, uncovered, for about 15 minutes.

6. Slit open each pepper on one side, taking care not to cut through the stem, and carefully remove the seeds and veins. Fill with the meat filling.

7. Beat the egg whites until stiff. Lightly beat the yolks and fold them into the whites.

8. Heat the lard or oil to smoking point in a heavy frying pan. Dust each pepper evenly with flour, then coat it in the beaten eggs and fry until golden brown on all sides, turning carefully. Drain on kitchen paper.

9. Remove the cinnamon stick from the tomato sauce, pour the sauce into a deep warmed serving dish and add the hot peppers. Sprinkle with parsley and serve immediately.

10. As a variation, you can stuff the peppers with thin slices of Mozzarella cheese.

Serves 4

2 Peppers with Vinegar

This dish can be served warm as a vegetable or chilled and served with shredded lettuce as a garnish for tacos, enchiladas or other tortilla dishes.

Ingredients

3 red peppers, roasted, peeled and seeded
3 green peppers, roasted, peeled and seeded
120 ml/4 fl oz/½ cup olive oil
3 cloves garlic, crushed
1 large onion, sliced
75 ml/5 tbsp white or red wine vinegar
2.5 ml/½ tsp dried oregano
Salt and freshly ground black pepper

Method

1.   Cut the peppers into thin strips or wedge shapes. Heat the oil in a heavy frying pan and fry the garlic until golden. Remove from the pan and discard.

2.   Add the peppers and onion and fry until the onion is translucent. Remove from the heat and cool slightly.

3.   Add the wine vinegar and oregano and season to taste with salt and pepper. Serve warm, or cover and chill.

Serves 4 to 6

3 Corn Pudding

Ingredients

6 corn cobs
250 ml/8 fl oz/1 cup milk
100 g/4 oz/1 cup butter at room temperature
5 eggs, separated
5 ml/1 tsp salt
A pinch of sugar
100 g/4 oz mild cheese, grated
75 ml/5 tbsp breadcrumbs
175 ml/6 fl oz/¾ cup double cream, whipped

Method

1. Cut the kernels off the ears of corn, then scrape the ears to collect the milky juice. Purée the kernels with enough juice to make a smooth purée and reserve any remaining milk.

2. Cream the butter, then add the egg yolks one at a time, mixing well after each addition. Stir in the salt, sugar, cheese, corn and reserved milk.

3. Beat the egg whites until stiff then fold them into the mixture.

4. Heavily butter a large ovenproof dish and sprinkle evenly with breadcrumbs. Pour in the pudding and bake in a preheated oven at 180°C/350°F/gas mark 4 for about 45 minutes until firm. Serve immediately with whipped cream.

Serves 4

Peppers in Walnut Sauce

Ingredients

350 g/12 oz pork shoulder, cubed
15 ml/1 tbsp lard or corn or safflower oil
1 clove garlic, finely chopped
1 small onion, finely chopped
350 g/12 oz tomatoes, skinned, seeded and puréed
25 g/1 oz/¼ cup sultanas
25 g/1 oz/¼ cup flaked almonds
15 ml/1 tbsp acitron or candied pineapple
A pinch of ground cinnamon
Salt and freshly ground black pepper
1 pear, peeled and diced
1 peach, peeled and diced
Sugar (optional)

For the sauce:
225 g/8 oz/2 cups walnut pieces
100 g/4 oz/1 cup flaked almonds
175 g/6 oz cream cheese or feta cheese
300 ml/½ pt/1 ¼ cups double cream
Salt or sugar (optional)

8 green peppers, roasted and peeled
15 ml/1 tbsp corn or safflower oil
15 ml/1 tbsp finely chopped fresh parsley
Seeds of 1 pomegranate (optional)

Method

1. To make the filling, place the pork in a saucepan, cover with salted water, bring to the boil, partially cover and cook for about 45 minutes until tender. Drain the meat and reserve the broth.

2.   Heat the lard or oil in a heavy frying pan and fry the garlic and onion until the onion is translucent. Add the meat and cook, stirring, until the meat is lightly browned.

3.   Stir in the tomato purée, sultanas, almonds, acitron or candied pineapple and cinnamon. Season to taste with salt and pepper and simmer for 10 minutes until thickened.

4.   Add the pears and peaches and simmer for a further 5 minutes. Add sugar to taste, if using, set aside and keep warm.

5.   To make the sauce, blend the walnuts, almonds and cheese with just enough cream to make a smooth pure, then add the remaining cream to make a smooth sauce. Season to taste with salt or sugar, if using. Refrigerate for at least 30 minutes.

6.   Cut the peppers open on the side, keeping the stem portion intact, and carefully remove the seeds and veins. Dry on kitchen paper and stuff with the filling.

7.   Heat the oil in a large frying pan over a low heat and add the peppers. Cover and cook for 3 minutes, then turn the peppers and cook for a further 3 minutes until the peppers are heated through but not browned. Drain on kitchen paper and place in a shallow warmed serving dish. Pour over the walnut sauce, sprinkle with parsley and garnish with pomegranate seeds, if using. Serve immediately.

Serves 4

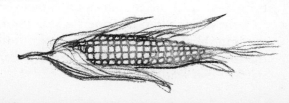

5 | Stuffed Avocados

Ingredients

For the filling:
350 g/12 oz pork shoulder, cubed
15 ml/1 tbsp lard or corn or safflower oil
15 ml/1 tbsp finely chopped onion
225 g/8 oz tomatoes, skinned, seeded and puréed
A pinch of ground cinnamon
A pinch of ground cloves
A pinch of ground cumin
Salt and freshly ground black pepper
10 ml/2 tsp capers
10 ml/2 tsp finely chopped fresh parsley

For the sauce:
15 ml/1 tbsp olive oil
350 g/12 oz tomatoes, skinned, seeded and puréed

2 large avocados, peeled and halved
2 eggs, beaten
Melted lard or corn or safflower oil to 1 cm/½ in depth

Method

1. To make the filling, place the pork in a saucepan and just cover with salted water. Bring to the boil, partially cover and simmer for about 45 minutes until tender. Let the meat cool in the stock, then remove the meat and shred it with a fork. Reserve 200 ml/7 fl oz/scant 1 cup of stock.

2. Heat the lard or oil to smoking point in a heavy frying pan and fry the pork and onion until lightly browned. Add the tomatoes and spices and season to taste with salt and pepper. Cook over a medium heat, stirring, for 4 minutes until the mixture is thickened. Stir in the capers and parsley. Set aside.

3. To make the sauce, heat the olive oil in a heavy saucepan, add the tomato purée and cook over a medium heat, stirring, for about 5 minutes. Add the reserved stock and simmer, uncovered, for 10 minutes until slightly thickened. Season to taste with salt. Pour into a shallow serving dish and keep warm.

4. Spoon the filling into the centres of the avocados and press down with the back of a spoon so that it is level with the top.

5. Mix a pinch of salt into the beaten eggs in a deep bowl. Heat the lard or oil almost to smoking point. With a slotted spoon, dip each avocado into the eggs so that it is completely coated. Fry the avocados, filling side down, until lightly browned, then turn carefully and brown the other side. Place the avocados in the tomato sauce and serve immediately.

6. As a variation, you can substitute 225 g/8 oz grated Mozzarella or mild Cheddar cheese for the meat filling.

Serves 4

6 Courgettes with Corn

Ingredients

1 kg/2 ¼ lb pork spareribs
60 ml/4 tbsp lard or corn or safflower oil
3 green peppers, roasted, peeled, seeded and cut into strips
350 g/12 oz tomatoes, roasted and skinned
1 onion, chopped
1 clove garlic
225 g/8 oz small corn cobs
675 g/1 ½ lb small courgettes, cubed
Salt and freshly ground black pepper
225 g/8 oz Mozzarella cheese, thinly sliced

Method

1. Place the spareribs in a saucepan with enough water to cover, bring to the boil, partially cover and simmer for about 45 minutes until tender. Remove the spareribs from the pan and dry on kitchen paper. If you have more than 1 litre/1 ¾ pts/4 ½ cups of stock, boil until the liquid is reduced. If you have less, add a little water.

2. Heat the lard or oil almost to smoking point in a heavy frying pan and fry the spareribs until lightly browned, adding the pepper strips for the last few minutes of cooking. Remove from the heat and drain off excess oil.

3. Purée the tomatoes with the onion and garlic. Add the tomato mixture to the pan with the corn and courgettes and cook over a medium heat, stirring, for 5 minutes until the sauce has thickened. Add the stock and season to taste with salt and pepper. Simmer, uncovered, for 20 minutes until the

vegetables are tender and the sauce has thickened. Adjust the seasoning to taste.

4.   Place the meat and vegetables in a large shallow serving dish and garnish with the slices of cheese. Serve immediately.

Serves 4

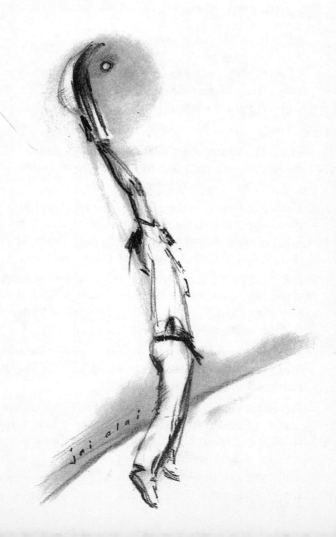

7 Courgette Pudding

Ingredients

750 g/1 ½ lb small courgettes, grated
Salt
15 ml/1 tbsp lard or corn or safflower oil
2 green peppers, roasted, peeled, seeded and cut into thin strips
225 g/8 oz tomatoes, skinned and chopped
2 eggs, separated
75 ml/5 tbsp double cream
100 g/4 oz Mozzarella cheese, thinly sliced
250 ml/8 fl oz/1 cup soured cream

Method

1. Place the courgettes in a colander, sprinkle with salt and leave to drain for about 30 minutes. Press out any excess moisture.

2. Heat the lard or oil in a heavy frying pan and fry the peppers and tomatoes over a medium heat for 4 minutes. Season to taste with salt. Remove from the heat and cool to room temperature.

3. Beat the egg whites until stiff. Beat the egg yolks until pale then mix in the cream and cooled tomato mixture. Fold in the egg whites and season to taste with salt.

4. Pour into a heavily buttered ovenproof casserole and bake in a preheated oven at 180°C/350°F/gas mark 4 for 30 minutes until set.

5. Arrange the cheese evenly over the top of the pudding and return to the oven for a few minutes until the cheese has slightly melted. Season the soured cream with salt, pour it over the pudding and serve immediately.

Serves 4

Beans and Rice

Almost as common in Mexico as corn, beans combine with corn or rice to make a complete protein, so are ideal to serve together. Chilli con Carne (page 118), Frontier Beans (page 119) and Black Beans Yucatan-Style (page 120) are all sufficiently substantial to serve as main courses.

All beans must be boiled steadily for 15 minutes during cooking to destroy the toxins they contain.

1 Mexican-Style Beans

Ingredients

450 g/1 lb/2 ⅔ cups red, kidney, pinto or black beans
1.5 litres/2 ¾ pts/6 cups water
2 small onions
45 ml/3 tbsp lard
10 ml/2 tsp salt

Method

1. Place the beans and water in a flameproof earthenware casserole. Halve one onion and chop the other. Add the halved onion to the pot, bring slowly to the boil, cover and boil for 15 minutes, then reduce to a simmer. When the beans begin to wrinkle, add 15 ml/1 tbsp of lard and simmer for about 1½ hours until the beans are tender, adding salt without stirring just before the end of cooking.

2. Heat the remaining lard in another pan and fry the chopped onion until translucent. Add to the cooked beans and simmer, uncovered, until the liquid has reduced slightly.

Serves 4 to 6

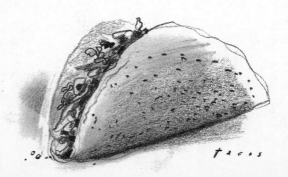

2 | Refried Beans

Ingredients

120 ml/4 fl oz/½ cup lard or corn or safflower oil
750 g/1 ½ lb/4 cups Mexican-Style Beans (page 116)
Bean stock
Grated Mozzarella or mild Cheddar cheese, fried and
crumbled
Chorizo sausage or thin slices of avocado

Method

1. Heat the lard or oil in a heavy frying pan over a high heat. Add the beans in small amounts with a little bean stock, mashing them quickly to a coarse paste with a masher or large spoon.

2. Reduce the heat to medium and cook until the beans begin to dry out and pull away from the sides of the pan in a mass. Tilt the pan from side to side until the beans can be rolled out of the pan like an omelette. Serve very hot with any one or more of the suggested garnishes.

Serves 6

3 | Chilli con Carne

Ingredients

225 g/8 oz pork shoulder, cubed
Salt
2 fresh chillies, toasted and seeded
2 cloves garlic
½ onion, quartered
A pinch of cumin seeds
A pinch of dried oregano
15 ml/1 tbsp lard or corn or safflower oil
15 ml/1 tbsp plain flour
750 g/12 oz/2 cups Mexican-Style Beans (page 116)
Crumbled natural cream cheese (optional)
Chopped onion (optional)

Method

1. Place the meat in a large saucepan with enough salted water to cover, bring to the boil, partially cover and simmer for about 45 minutes until tender. Drain the meat and reserve 250 ml/8 fl oz/ 1 cup of stock.

2. Purée the chillies with the garlic and onion. Grind the cumin seeds, then add to the purée with the oregano, adding enough of the reserved stock to make a smooth sauce.

3. Heat the lard or oil in a large frying pan and cook the flour, stirring, until it begins to brown. Add the chilli mixture and cook over a medium heat, stirring, for about 5 minutes. Add the cooked meat and reserved broth, season to taste with salt, cover and simmer for about 30 minutes until slightly thickened.

4.   Combine this mixture with the cooked beans and
       heat together for several minutes to combine the
       flavours. Serve sprinkled with cheese or chopped
       onion, if using.

Serves 4

 Frontier Beans

Ingredients

4 rashers bacon
1 green pepper, roasted, peeled, seeded and chopped
225 g/8 oz tomatoes, skinned, seeded and chopped
750 g/12 oz/2 cups Mexican-Style Beans (page 116)
1 chorizo sausage, thinly sliced
*100 g/4 oz Mozzarella or natural cream cheese, thinly
sliced*
Sour gherkins or green or black olives

Method

1.   Brown the bacon in a heavy frying pan. Remove
       and drain on kitchen paper. Cook the pepper and
       tomatoes in the bacon fat until tender. Add the
       beans with their stock and the chorizo.

2.   Simmer, uncovered, until the broth has thickened
       slightly and the chorizo is cooked through. Serve
       very hot, garnished with the bacon and cheese and
       the gherkins or olives.

Serves 4

Black Beans Yucatan-Style

You can save the stock from this dish to make Black Rice if you like. To serve it as a main course, increase the amount of pork to 750 g/1½ lb.

Ingredients

350 g/12 oz/2 cups black beans
10 ml/2 tsp sea salt
225 g/8 oz pork shoulder or spareribs, cubed
2.5 ml/½ tsp salt
60 ml/4 tbsp lard or corn or safflower oil
1 onion, finely chopped
1 clove garlic, crushed
5 ml/1 tsp chilli powder
Salt
15 ml/1 tbsp olive oil
50 g/2 oz mature Cheddar cheese, grated

Method

1. Place the beans in a flameproof earthenware casserole with enough water to cover. Bring slowly to the boil, cover and boil for 15 minutes, then reduce to a simmer for about 1 ½ hours until the beans are tender, adding salt without stirring just before the end of cooking.

2. Meanwhile, place the meat and salt in a saucepan and barely cover with water. Bring to the boil then simmer, uncovered, for about 45 minutes until the meat is tender. Allow the meat to cool in the stock, then drain the meat and measure 500 ml/18 fl oz/ 2¼ cups of stock. Add a little water or reduce by boiling, if necessary.

3.   When the beans are tender, drain them and reserve the stock. Rinse in cold water.

4.   Heat the lard or oil in a heavy frying pan and cook the onion and garlic until the onion is translucent. Add the beans and cook, stirring, for several minutes. Add the pork, stock and chilli powder and season to taste with salt. Simmer, uncovered, until slightly thickened. Sprinkle with olive oil and serve garnished with cheese.

Serves 4 to 6

6 Mexican-Style Rice

Ingredients

350 g/12 oz/1 ½ cups long-grain rice
60 ml/4 tbsp lard or corn or safflower oil
225 g/8 oz tomatoes, skinned, seeded and puréed
30 ml/2 tbsp finely chopped onion
250 ml/8 fl oz/1 cup cold water
2.5 ml/½ tsp salt
225 g/8 oz shelled peas
450 ml/¾ pt/2 cups hot chicken stock
2 chorizo sausages
5 ml/1 tsp finely chopped fresh parsley
2 avocados, peeled and thinly sliced

Method

1. Soak the rice in hot water to cover for 15 minutes. Rinse in cold water until the water runs clear then put in a sieve to drain.

2. Heat the lard or oil and fry the rice, stirring constantly, until opaque. Tip the pan and collect any excess lard or oil with a spoon; discard.

3. Add the tomato purée and onion and cook over a high heat, stirring, until the rice is almost dry. Add the cold water, salt and peas and simmer, uncovered, until the rice is again almost dry.

4. Add the hot stock, cover and simmer for about 30 minutes until the rice is dry and the grains are separate.

5. Meanwhile, remove the chorizos from their casings and fry in a heavy frying pan until browned and crumbly.

6. To serve, transfer the rice to a warmed serving dish, sprinkle with chorizo and parsley and garnish with slices of avocado.

Serves 4

 # White Rice

Ingredients

350 g/12 oz/1 ½ cups long-grain rice
45 ml/3 tbsp lard or corn or safflower oil
1 small onion, chopped
2 cloves garlic, crushed
750 ml/1¼ pts/3 cups hot water
1 sprig of parsley
1 fresh chilli, seeded and chopped (optional)
5 ml/1 tsp salt

Method

1. Soak the rice in hot water to cover for 15 minutes. Rinse in cold water until the water runs clear then put in a sieve to drain.

2. Heat the lard or oil in a heavy flameproof casserole with a lid and cook the rice with the onion and garlic, stirring constantly, until the rice is opaque. Tip the pan and collect any excess lard or oil with a spoon; discard.

3. Add the hot water, parsley, chilli if using and salt, stirring once. Cover and cook over a low heat for about 30 minutes until the rice is spongy.

Serves 4

Rice with Fried Meat and Bananas

Ingredients

1 quantity White Rice (page 123)
60 ml/4 tbsp lard
15 ml/1 tbsp finely chopped onion
450 g/1 lb beef, finely chopped
225 g/8 oz tomatoes, skinned, seeded and puréed
15 ml/1 tbsp chopped fresh parsley
25 g/1 oz/¼ cup sultanas, plumped in water
25 g/1 oz/¼ cup flaked almonds
Salt and freshly ground black pepper
60 ml/4 tbsp corn or safflower oil
4 firm bananas, halved lengthways

Method

1.   Prepare the white rice and set aside.

2.   Heat the lard in a heavy frying pan and fry the onion and meat until the meat is well browned. Add the tomato and parsley and simmer for 5 minutes. Add the sultanas and almonds and season to taste with salt and pepper.

3.   Heat the oil in a heavy frying pan and fry the bananas slowly until golden brown, turning carefully.

4.   Serve the rice, meat and bananas on separate plates so that the guests can combine them to taste.

Serves 6

9 | Green Rice

Ingredients

350 g/12 oz/1 ½ cups long-grain rice
60 ml/4 tbsp lard or corn or safflower oil
3 green peppers, roasted, peeled and seeded
1 onion, chopped
1 clove garlic
1 litre/1 3/4 pts/4 ¼ cups hot chicken stock
2.5 ml/½ tsp salt
40 g/1 ½ oz/3 tbsp butter
50 g/2 oz Mozzarella or natural cream cheese, thinly
sliced

Method

1. Soak the rice in hot water to cover for 15 minutes.
    Rinse in cold water until the water runs clear then
    put in a sieve to drain.

2. Heat the lard or oil in a heavy frying pan and cook
    the rice, stirring, until opaque. Tip the pan and
    collect any excess lard or oil with a spoon; discard.

3. Purée the peppers with the onion and garlic and
    add this to the rice. Cook over a medium heat
    until the rice becomes almost dry.

4. Add the hot stock and salt, cover and cook over a
    low heat for about 15 minutes until the rice is
    again almost dry. Dot with the butter, then leave
    on a low heat for about 15 minutes until the rice is
    fully dry and the grains are separate. Serve
    garnished with the cheese.

Serves 4

10 | Prawn Rice

If you are using cooked prawns for this recipe, there is no need to blanch them in the hot oil.

Ingredients

350 g/12 oz/1 ½ cups long-grain rice
90 ml/6 tbsp lard or corn or safflower oil
450 g/1 lb uncooked prawns
2 cloves garlic, crushed
750 g/1 ½ lb tomatoes, skinned, seeded and puréed
1 small onion, finely chopped
750 ml/1 ¼ pts/3 cups hot water
Salt
3 sprigs of coriander, finely chopped (optional)
1 sprig of mint, finely chopped (optional)

Method

1.   Soak the rice in hot water to cover for 15 minutes. Rinse in cold water until the water runs clear then put in a sieve to drain.

2.   Heat half the lard or oil in a heavy frying pan and fry the prawns for about 1 minute. Drain on kitchen paper.

3.   Heat the remaining lard or oil in a flameproof casserole with a lid and fry the garlic until lightly browned, then remove and discard. Add the rice and cook, stirring constantly, until the rice is opaque. Tip the pan and collect any excess lard or oil with a spoon; discard.

4.   Add the tomatoes and onion and cook over a medium heat until the rice is almost dry. Add the water, salt, coriander and mint, if using, stirring once, then simmer over a low heat for about 20 minutes.

5.   Add the prawns, stir once and continue to cook for
        a further 5 to 10 minutes until the rice is almost
        dry.

Serves 4

11 | Yellow Rice

Ingredients

> 350 g/12 oz/1 ½ cups long-grain rice
> 45 ml/3 tbsp lard or corn or safflower oil
> 1 onion, finely chopped
> 2 cloves garlic, crushed
> 175 g/6 oz tomatoes, skinned, seeded and puréed
> 750 ml/1 ¼ pts/3 cups hot chicken stock or water
> 2.5 ml/½ tsp salt
> 1 fresh chilli, seeded and finely chopped (optional)

Method

1.   Soak the rice in hot water to cover for 15 minutes.
        Rinse in cold water until the water runs clear then
        put in a sieve to drain.

2.   Heat the lard or oil in a heavy flameproof
        casserole with a lid. Cook the rice with the onion
        and garlic, stirring continuously, until the rice is
        golden. Tip the pan and collect any excess lard or
        oil with a spoon; discard.

3.   Add the tomatoes and cook, stirring, for a further
        3 minutes then add the stock or water and the salt.
        Add the chilli, if using, bring to the boil, stirring
        once, then cover and simmer for 30 minutes until
        almost dry.

Serves 4

12 | Black Rice

Ingredients

350 g/12 oz/1 ½ cups long-grain rice
45 ml/3 tbsp lard or corn or safflower oil
1 small onion, finely chopped
3 cloves garlic, crushed
750 ml/1 ¼ pts/3 cups hot stock from
  Black Beans Yucatan-Style (page 120)
Salt
New peas, artichoke hearts, shrimps or chopped ham,
  pork or beef (optional)

Method

1. Soak the rice in hot water to cover for 15 minutes.
    Rinse in cold water until the water runs clear then
    put in a sieve to drain.

2. Heat the lard or oil in a heavy flameproof
    casserole with a lid and cook the rice with the
    onion and garlic, stirring constantly, until the rice
    is opaque. Tip the pan and collect any excess lard
    or oil with a spoon; discard.

3. Add the hot bean broth and salt to taste. Add one
    or more of the optional ingredients, bring to the
    boil, stirring once, then cover and simmer for 30
    minutes until almost dry.

Serves 4

Salads

Salads are perfect accompaniments to tortilla dishes. Don't forget the simplest of Mexican salads: sliced tomatoes and avocados, alone or on a bed of lettuce or lettuce with onion slices and radishes. For a dressing, use a light oil and white wine vinegar mixture, or Tomato Sauce (page 155). Guacamole (page 18) on a bed of chopped lettuce also makes an excellent salad.

Cauliflower Salad

Ingredients

> 1 small cauliflower
> 5 ml/1 tsp mustard powder
> 30 ml/2 tbsp fresh orange juice
> 1 egg yolk
> 150 ml/¼ pt/⅔ cups corn or safflower oil
> 1 fresh chilli, seeded and chopped
> 30 ml/2 tbsp white wine vinegar
> 2.5 ml/½ tsp dried oregano
> Salt and freshly ground white pepper
> 5 lettuce leaves

Method

1. Cook the cauliflower in a little boiling salted water until just tender, then drain, cool and separate into florets.

2. Dissolve the mustard in the orange juice, then beat in the egg yolk. Gradually add the oil, beating continuously, then mix in the chilli, wine vinegar and oregano and season to taste with salt and pepper.

3. Arrange the lettuce leaves in a serving bowl with the cauliflower on top and pour over the dressing.

Serves 4

2 Marinated Courgettes

Ingredients

45 ml/3 tbsp olive oil
450 g/1 lb courgettes, thinly sliced
4 cloves garlic, crushed
1 onion, halved
Salt and freshly ground black pepper
150 ml/¼ pt/⅔ cup red wine vinegar
5 ml/1 tsp dried oregano or sage
6 lettuce leaves, chopped
½ red onion, sliced into rings

Method

1. Heat the oil in a frying pan, add the courgettes, garlic and onion and cook over a medium heat, stirring, for 5 minutes.

2. Reduce to a low heat, season to taste with salt and pepper, cover and simmer for 10 minutes, then uncover and simmer for a further 4 minutes until the liquid has evaporated, adding a little more olive oil if necessary.

3. Place the courgettes in a shallow dish and add enough wine vinegar to half cover. Sprinkle with oregano or sage, cover with kitchen foil and refrigerate for 4 or 5 days, stirring twice a day.

4. Arrange the chopped lettuce leaves in a serving dish and top with the courgettes. Garnish with onion rings to serve.

Serves 4

Marinated Vegetable Salad

Ingredients

A pinch of cumin seeds
10 ml/2 tsp chilli powder
1 clove garlic, crushed
175 ml/6 fl oz/¾ cup white wine vinegar
750 g/1 ½ lb small courgettes, sliced
350 g/12 oz small new potatoes, sliced
175 g/6 oz shelled peas
1 small sprig of thyme
1 bay leaf
Salt
½ onion, sliced into rings
60 ml/4 tbsp olive oil
100 g/4 oz Mozzarella cheese, sliced

Method

1. Grind the cumin seeds in a mortar and pestle then blend with the chilli, garlic and wine vinegar to a smooth paste.

2. Cook the courgettes, potatoes and peas separately in boiling salted water until just tender then drain. Combine the cooked vegetables in a bowl with the chilli mixture, thyme, bay leaf and salt to taste.

3. Place the onion rings in a separate bowl and cover with cold water and 5 ml/1 tsp of salt. Cover both bowls tightly and refrigerate for several hours or overnight.

4. Just before serving, remove the bay leaf from the vegetables, add the oil, and arrange them in a

shallow serving dish. Garnish with the drained onion rings and the cheese.

Serves 4

 # Beetroot Salad

Ingredients

4 medium beetroots
120 ml/4 fl oz/½ cup dry sherry
5 ml/1 tsp sugar
2.5 ml/½ tsp salt
15 ml/1 tbsp white wine vinegar
Salt and freshly ground black pepper.
15 ml/1 tbsp chopped fresh parsley

Method

1. Cover the beetroots with boiling salted water and simmer until just tender. Drain and allow to cool, then peel and dice and place in a mixing bowl.

2. Mix together the sherry, sugar, salt and wine vinegar and stir the mixture into the beetroots. Season to taste with salt and pepper. Cover and refrigerate for at least 30 minutes.

3. Place in a shallow serving dish and sprinkle with chopped parsley.

Serves 4

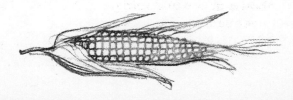

Cucumber and Artichoke Salad

Ingredients

450 g/1 lb Jerusalem artichokes, peeled
1 small cucumber
1 red onion, thinly sliced
30 ml/2 tbsp fresh lime juice
2.5 ml/½ tsp grated lime rind
1 clove garlic, crushed
A pinch of salt
A pinch of chilli powder
45 ml/3 tbsp corn or safflower oil
1 lettuce

Method

1.   Cut the artichokes in half lengthways then cut them into thin slices. Cut the cucumber in half lengthways, scoop out and discard the seeds. Cut the halves into thick slices.

2.   Mix together the artichokes, cucumber and onion.

3.   Mix together the lime juice and rind, garlic, salt and chilli powder. Gradually whisk in the oil until the dressing is thoroughly blended.

4.   Pour the dressing over the salad and toss lightly. Cover and refrigerate for 2 hours.

5.   Line a salad bowl with lettuce leaves, spoon in the salad and serve.

Serves 6

Desserts and Cakes

*More than any other category of
food, Mexican desserts reflect the
European influence. The Spanish
brought sugar, wheat flour,
chicken eggs, milks, cream and
almonds to Mexico, and many of
the desserts popular today were
perfected in convents by Spanish
nuns. Remember that fresh fruits
such as pineapples, mangoes,
papayas, bananas and oranges,
sliced and sprinkled with sugar
and lemon or lime juice or rum
are always good desserts for
Mexican meals.*

Fried Plantains or Bananas

Ingredients

4 ripe plantains or 4 firm bananas
50 g/2 oz/¼ cup butter
30 ml/2 tbsp dark brown sugar
30 ml/2 tbsp dark rum
Freshly ground nutmeg
300 ml/½ pt/1 ¼ cups double cream

Method

1.   Peel the plantains or bananas and cut them in half lengthways. Heat the butter in a heavy frying pan and fry the plantains or bananas over a low heat until they are very tender, turning carefully.

2.   Sprinkle with sugar, rum and nutmeg to taste and serve hot with cream.

Serves 4

2 Peaches with Almond Sauce

Ingredients

4 peaches
225 g/8 oz sugar
500 ml/18 fl oz/2 ¼ cups water
1 stick cinnamon
50 g/2 oz/½ cup ground almonds
175 ml/6 fl oz/¾ cup double cream
2 egg yolks, lightly beaten

Method

1. Plunge the peaches in boiling water for 15 seconds, then cool slightly in cold water and slip off the skins.

2. Mix the sugar and water in a saucepan and bring to the boil, stirring to dissolve the sugar. Add the cinnamon and peaches and simmer, turning the peaches if necessary, until they are tender. Remove the peaches with a slotted spoon and arrange them on a serving dish.

3. Remove the cinnamon and boil the syrup until it is reduced to about 200 ml/7 fl oz/scant 1 cup. Mix in the ground almonds and cream and simmer for 3 minutes then remove from the heat.

4. Mix 30 ml/2 tbsp of the hot liquid into the egg yolks, then stir them into the syrup. Bring to the boil and cook for 3 minutes, stirring with a whisk. Allow the sauce to cool to room temperature then pour over the peaches to serve.

Serves 4

3 | Simple Flan

This classic Mexican flan is not a pastry, but a delicious type of set custard cooked on top of the stove.

Ingredients

> *225 g/8 oz/1 cup sugar*
> *3 egg yolks*
> *3 eggs*
> *500 ml/18 fl oz/2 ¼ cups milk*
> *15 ml/1 tbsp cornflour*
> *30 ml/2 tbsp water*
> *5 ml/1 tsp vanilla essence*

Method

1. Place half the sugar in a heavy pan over a high heat and stir constantly with a wooden spoon until the sugar begins to foam and turn a deep golden brown. Be careful not to let it burn. Immediately pour the caramel into a flan or pudding mould, turning it quickly so that the caramel coats the bottom and sides. Allow to cool.

2. Beat the egg yolks and eggs until they thicken slightly.

3. Place the milk in a saucepan and bring to the boil over a medium heat and add the remaining sugar. Dissolve the cornflour in the water and add this to the milk. Gradually beat the milk into the beaten eggs. Add the vanilla essence and mix well.

4. Pour the custard mixture into the mould. Butter the underside of a tightly fitting lid and cover the mould so that it is airtight, or cover with a layer of buttered kitchen foil and a lid. Place the mould in a pan with water to come about half-way up the

sides. Simmer gently for about 2 hours, taking care that the water does not splash into the mould and topping up with boiling water as necessary. When ready, a knife inserted into the centre will come out clean.

5. Remove the flan from the pan and cool it to room temperature before serving.

6. There are many variations to this simple flan.

For an Orange Flan, use freshly squeezed and strained orange juice instead of milk and grated orange peel to taste instead of vanilla essence.

For Pineapple Flan, use pineapple juice instead of milk and allow the pineapple juice to cool slightly before adding the cornflour and mixing with the eggs.

For Coconut Flan, put 100 g/4 oz of desiccated coconut, 120 ml/4 fl oz/½ cup of water and 100 g/ 4 oz/½ cup of sugar in a saucepan and simmer until the coconut becomes translucent. Follow the basic recipe and add the coconut mixture to the boiled milk with the remaining sugar.

For Nut Flan, add 175 g/6 oz ground mixed nuts to the boiled milk with the sugar.

Serves 4

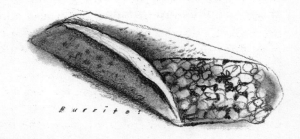

Burritos!

4 Celaya Milk Cream

This is a thick, very sweet confection that is eaten with a spoon or served as a topping for vanilla ice cream or a filling for pancakes. The goats' milk gives it a musky flavour and taste, but it can be made with cows' milk if you prefer. It will keep almost indefinitely in the refrigerator in tightly sealed jars.

Ingredients

1.5 litres/2 ½ pts/6 cups goats' milk
1.5 litres/2 ½ pts/6 cups cows' milk
2.5 ml/½ tsp bicarbonate of soda
5 ml/1 tsp cornflour
750 g/1 ½ lb/3 cups sugar

Method

1. Place the goats' milk and most of the cows' milk in a large, heavy saucepan and bring to the boil. Mix the remaining milk with the bicarbonate of soda and cornflour and add it to the pan slowly, stirring well. Stir in the sugar until it dissolves.

2. Boil the mixture until it has thickened to the consistency of double cream. Continue to boil, stirring constantly, until the mixture has thickened so that it forms a ribbon when poured from a spoon. Cool before serving.

Makes 1.5 litres/2 ½ pts/6 cups

5 Mexican Rice Pudding

Ingredients

25 g/1 oz/¼ cup sultanas
225 g/8 oz/1 cup long-grain rice
500 ml/18 fl oz/2 ¼ cups water
A pinch of salt
2 strips of lemon rind
500 ml/18 fl oz/2 ¼ cups milk
1 stick cinnamon
175 g/6 oz/¾ cup sugar
2 egg yolks, lightly beaten
Freshly ground nutmeg

Method

1. Soak the sultanas in a little water to plump them. Soak the rice in hot water to cover for 15 minutes. Rinse in cold water until the water runs clear then place in a sieve to drain.

2. Bring the water to the boil in a heavy saucepan and add the salt, lemon rind and rice. Cover and simmer for about 20 minutes until almost dry.

3. Heat the milk with the cinnamon over a low heat until almost boiling then stir into the rice with the sugar and simmer, uncovered, until most of the milk is absorbed.

4. Remove the cinnamon stick, remove from the heat and allow to cool slightly. Stir in the egg yolks and return to the heat. Cook over a low heat, stirring occasionally to prevent sticking, until the pudding is slightly thickened.

5. Mix in the drained sultanas, pour into a serving dish and serve sprinkled with freshly ground nutmeg.

Serves 4

Fritters in Syrup

These fritters, or *buñuelos*, can be served with Walnut and Honey Sauce (page 157) instead of the aniseed syrup, or simply sprinkled with ground cinnamon and sugar.

Ingredients

> 450 g/1 lb/2 cups dark brown sugar
> 450 ml/3/4 pt/2 cups water
> 10 ml/2 tsp aniseed
> 450 g/1 lb/4 cups plain flour
> 5 ml/1 tsp baking powder
> 2.5 ml/½ tsp salt
> 2 eggs
> 250 ml/8 fl oz/1 cup corn or safflower oil

Method

1. To make the syrup, dissolved the brown sugar in half the water over a low heat. Add half the aniseed and bring to the boil. Continue boiling until the syrup thickens slightly, then strain to remove the aniseed and set aside to cool.

2. Bring the remaining water and aniseed to the boil then remove from the heat and leave to cool.

3. Sift the flour with the baking powder and salt. Add the eggs and enough aniseed water to make a firm dough. Knead the dough well until smooth. Divide into 18 balls and roll out on floured surface into circles about 1 cm/½ in thick. Leave the dough on a floured surface for about 30 minutes to dry out slightly.

4. Heat the oil to smoking point in a heavy frying pan and fry the fritters until puffed and golden, then drain on kitchen paper. Serve warm, with the syrup poured over or passed separately.

Makes 18

7 Walnut Biscuits

Ingredients

100 g/4 oz/½ cup butter
75 g/3 oz/⅓ cup sugar
100 g/4 oz/½ cup walnuts, ground
100 g/4 oz/1 cup plain flour
Sifted icing sugar

Method

1. Cream together the butter and sugar. Mix in the ground walnuts and flour. Chill the dough for 1 hour.

2. Form the dough into a roll about 3 cm/1 in in diameter and slice into biscuits about 6 mm/¼ in thick. Place on greased baking sheets and bake in a preheated oven at 180°C/350°F/gas mark 4 for 15 minutes.

3. Allow to cool slightly, then dip in icing sugar before serving.

Makes 30 biscuits

8 | Easter Egg Bread

Ingredients

250 ml/8 fl oz/1 cup milk
150 g/5 oz/⅔ cup sugar
50 g/2 oz/¼ cup butter
50 g/2 oz/¼ cup lard
5 ml/1 tsp salt
15 g/½ oz dried yeast
120 ml/4 fl oz/½ cup warm water
550 g/1 lb 4 oz/5 cups plain flour
3 egg yolks
5 ml/1 tsp vanilla essence
1 egg white
15 ml/1 tbsp cold water
60 ml/4 tbsp raisins
45 ml/3 tbsp mixed peel
30 ml/2 tbsp sesame seeds

For the egg filling:
1 large egg
30 ml/2 tbsp sugar
15 ml/1 tbsp plain flour
2.5 ml/½ tsp vanilla essence

Method

1. Bring the milk to the boil then remove from the heat. Add the sugar, butter, lard and salt and stir until melted. Leave to stand at room temperature for 10 minutes.

2. Sprinkle the yeast on the warm water and leave to stand for 5 minutes.

3. Mix the milk and yeast mixtures in a large bowl and stir in half the flour. Mix well then beat until smooth. Cover and leave to stand for about 20 minutes until frothy.

4. Beat and egg yolks and vanilla essence into the batter. Add a further 175 g/6 oz/1½ cups of flour and beat until smooth and elastic. Gradually stir in as much of the remaining flour as needed to make a soft dough. Knead until smooth and elastic. Cover and leave in a warm place for about 1 hour until doubled in size.

5. Beat the egg white and cold water lightly.

6. Punch down the dough. Pinch off and reserve about one quarter. Knead the raisins into the remaining dough and shape it into a ball. Place on a greased baking sheet and flatten to a 25 cm/10 in circle. Brush lightly with egg white.

7. Divide the reserved dough into 24 pieces and roll each into a 13 cm/5 in long strand. Shape them into S shapes and arrange in two rings on the outside of the dough circle. Decorate the border with mixed peel. Cover loosely and leave in a warm place for about 45 minutes until doubled in size.

8. Brush the dough again with egg white and sprinkle with sesame seeds. Bake in a preheated oven at 180°C/350°F/gas mark 4 for 30 minutes, covering the top with foil if it begins to brown too much.

9. To make the egg filling, beat the egg until thick and pale then beat in the sugar, flour and vanilla essence until blended.

10. Spoon the egg filling on to the centre of the bread and return it to the oven for a further 10 minutes until the bread sounds hollow when tapped. Cool before serving.

Makes 1 x 33 cm/13 in round loaf

9 Garbanzo Cake

This is a firm-textured cake to serve with sliced fresh fruit such as oranges, pineapples or mangoes.

Ingredients

225 g/8 oz/1⅓ cups dry garbanzo beans
Salt
4 eggs, beaten
225 g/8 oz/1 cup sugar
2.5 ml/½ tsp baking powder
Grated rind of 1 large lemon
Sifted icing sugar

Method

1. Soak the beans overnight in water to cover.

2. Drain the beans and place in a saucepan with salted water to cover. Bring to the boil, cover and simmer for about 1½ hours until tender.

3. Rinse the beans under cold running water, rubbing them between your fingers to remove the skins.

4. Purée the beans then mix in the eggs, sugar, baking powder and lemon rind.

5. Butter a 23 cm/9 in cake tin or pudding or charlotte mould. Line the bottom with brown paper, buttered on both sides. Pour in the batter and bake in a preheated oven at 180°C/350°F/gas mark 4 for about 45 minutes until a skewer inserted into the centre comes out clean.

6. Cool to room temperature and sprinkle with icing sugar to serve.

Makes 1 x 23 cm/9 in cake

Drinks

Coffee and chocolate, in their distinctively Mexican versions, can be served with pastries at breakfast or in the afternoon, with egg dishes for brunch and after dinner. Serve Sangria (page 150) or Mexican beer with dinner, and Rompope (page 152) or a coffee liqueur as an after dinner drink.

1 Café de Olla

This is the traditional way of making coffee in Mexico in the olla, an earthenware pot.

Ingredients

1 litre/1 ¾ pts/4 ¼ cups water
Dark brown sugar
175 g/6 oz finely ground dark-roasted coffee

Method

1. Heat the water in a flameproof earthenware pot and add brown sugar to taste, stirring to dissolve.

2. Add the coffee and bring to the boil. Boil for 1 minute then remove from the heat.

3. Stir the coffee well then cover the pot and keep it warm until the coffee grounds have settled to the bottom. Pour through a fine sieve or a filter and serve in earthenware mugs.

4. As a variation, you can make Coffee with Milk by mixing in 3 parts hot milk to 1 part coffee.

Makes 1 litre/1 ¾ pts/4 ¼ cups

Enchilada

2 | Chocolate in Milk

Mexican chocolate is a mixture of chocolate, sugar, cinnamon and ground almonds and is sold packaged in tablets sectioned into triangles. It is traditionally heated in an olla, a deep earthenware pot, and whirled to a froth with a carved wooden utensil that is twirled between the palms of the hands. Serve Mexican chocolate for breakfast and in the late afternoon with sweet pastries.

Ingredients

175 g/6 oz dark chocolate
1 litre/1 ¾ pts/4 ¼ cups milk

Method

1. Put the chocolate and milk into a flameproof earthenware pot and bring to the boil, stirring occasionally to mix in the melting chocolate.

2. Remove from the heat for 1 minute, then return to the heat and bring to the boil again. Whisk or blend until frothy and serve in earthenware mugs.

3. As a variation, you can make Chocolate in Water. Replace the milk with water, melting the chocolate in half the water, then adding the remainder before bringing to the boil again and whisking.

Makes 1 litre / 1 ¾ pts / 4 ¼ cups

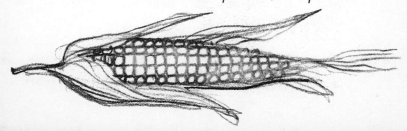

3 Sangria

Ingredients

450 ml/¾ pt/2 cups water
30 ml/2 tbsp sugar
450 ml/¾ pt/2 cups fresh orange juice
250 ml/8 fl oz/1 cup dry red wine
30 ml/2 tbsp fresh lemon juice
Coarsely crushed ice
Strips of lemon rind (optional)

Method

1. Place the water in a glass jug and add the sugar, stirring to dissolve. Add the orange juice, wine and lemon juice.

2. Serve poured over crushed ice and garnished with strips of lemon rind, if using.

    Makes 1 litre/1 ¾ pts/4 ¼ cups

4 Tequila Cocktail

Ingredients

1 egg white
150 ml/¼ pt/⅔ cup fresh lemon juice
45 ml/3 tbsp grenadine
250 ml/8 fl oz/1 cup white tequila
Coarsely crushed ice

Method

1. Place the egg white, lemon juice and grenadine in

a cocktail shaker or blender and shake or blend until well mixed.

2. Add the tequila and crushed ice and shake until very cold and frothy. Serve in a chilled glass jug.

Serves 4

5 Tequila Sunrise

Ingredients

Coarsely crushed ice
120 ml/4 fl oz/½ cup fresh orange juice
45 ml/3 tbsp white tequila
15 ml/1 tbsp grenadine

Method

1. Fill a large glass with ice, add the orange juice then the tequila. Stir with a long-handled spoon, then hold the back of the spoon on the surface of the drink and slowly pour the grenadine over.

Serves 1

tacos

6 | Rompope

Serve this rich egg nog drink in liqueur glasses after dinner or in the later afternoon accompanied with sweet pastries.

Ingredients

750 ml/1 ¼ pts/3 cups milk
225 g/8 oz/1 cup sugar
½ stick cinnamon
7 egg yolks
250 ml/8 fl oz/1 cup amber rum

Method

1. Place the milk, sugar and cinnamon in a saucepan and bring to the boil, stirring constantly. Boil steadily for 10 minutes or until the milk has reduced by about one-third, stirring frequently. Remove from the heat and cool to lukewarm.

2. Beat the egg yolks lightly and mix into the milk mixture. Return to the heat, bring back to the boil and simmer until slightly thickened.

3. Allow to cool a little, then stir in the rum. Whisk or blend until frothy. Allow to cool to room temperature then pour into sterilised glass bottles. Cap and store in the refrigerator where it will keep for several weeks.

Makes 1.5 litres/2½ pts/6 cups

7 Margarita Cocktail

Although its Mexican origins have been questioned, the margarita probably evolved from the Mexican custom of drinking straight tequila with salt and a wedge of lime. You can use any orange liqueur for the recipe.

Ingredients

1 wedge of lime
1 saucer of sea salt
45 ml/3 tbsp white tequila
15 ml/1 tbsp orange liqueur
30 ml/2 tbsp fresh lime juice
2.5 ml/½ tsp caster sugar
Coarsely crushed ice

Method

1. Rub the rim of a cocktail glass with the wedge of lime and reserve the lime. Dip the rim of the glass in the salt to coat the rim evenly.

2. Shake the tequila, orange liqueur, lime juice and sugar in a cocktail shaker or blend in a blender.

3. Serve strained or over ice, adding the reserved wedge of lime.

Serves 1

Enchilada

Sauces

The following sauces include both cooked and uncooked sauces as well as dessert recipes. The three guacamoles in the Appetiser section also make excellent sauces.

1 Tomato Sauce

This is the basic Mexican table sauce which is used with almost everything from tortillas to main dishes. With the addition of the wine vinegar it can also serve as a salad dressing. It is best when made fresh but can be stored in the refrigerator.

Ingredients

450 g/1 lb tomatoes, skinned, seeded and finely chopped
2 fresh chillies, seeded and finely chopped
1 onion, finely chopped
15 ml/1 tbsp finely chopped fresh coriander
30 ml/2 tbsp corn or safflower oil
30 ml/2 tbsp white wine vinegar (optional)
Salt and freshly ground black pepper

Method

1. Mix all the ingredients together well. Serve at the table to be added to food to taste.

Makes 750 ml/1 ¼ pts/3 cups

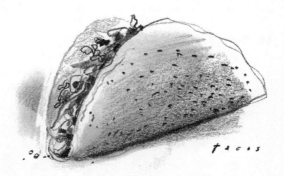

Tomatillo Sauce

This is the ideal sauce for tortilla dishes.

Ingredients

2 fresh chillies, seeded and chopped
Salt
450 g/1 lb tinned tomatillos, drained
1 onion, chopped
2 cloves garlic
15 ml/1 tbsp finely chopped fresh coriander
30 ml/2 tbsp lard or corn or safflower oil
A pinch of sugar

Method

1. Cook the chillies in a small amount of boiling salted water for about 10 minutes until tender, then drain.

2. Purée the tomatillos and chillies with the onion, garlic and coriander.

3. Heat the lard or oil in a heavy frying pan and cook the purée for about 4 minutes until slightly thickened. Season to taste with salt and sugar.

Makes 450 ml / ¾ pt / 2 cups

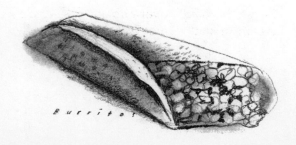

Burritos

Barbecue Sauce

This quantity of sauce is enough for at least 900 g/2 lb of meat or chicken.

Ingredients

900 g/2 lb tomatoes, roasted and skinned
1 clove garlic
1 onion, chopped
1 sprig of coriander (optional)
5 ml/1 tsp chilli powder
Salt

Method

1.   Purée the tomatoes with the garlic, onion and coriander, if using. Add enough water to make a smooth sauce and season to taste with chilli powder and salt.

Makes 750 ml/1 ¼ pts/3 cups

Walnut and Honey Sauce

Serve this sauce over chocolate, coffee or vanilla ice cream or with sweet fritters.

Ingredients

250 ml/8 fl oz/1 cup clear honey
50 g/2 oz/½ cup chopped walnuts

Method

1. Place the honey in a saucepan and bring to the boil. Boil for 3 minutes then remove from the heat.

2. Leave to cool slightly then mix in the nuts. Serve warm.

Makes 300 ml / ½ pt / ⅔ cup

5 | Banana Purée

This is an unusual sauce for grilled or baked fish, chicken or pork. It can also be used as a dessert sauce for fresh fruit or cake.

Ingredients

600 ml/1 pt/2 ½ cups hot milk
45 ml/3 tbsp sugar
2.5 ml/½ tsp salt
6 large ripe bananas, peeled and mashed
15 ml/1 tbsp butter
15 ml/1 tbsp grenadine

Method

1. Mix the milk, sugar, salt and bananas in a saucepan over a low heat. Cook, stirring constantly, until thickened.

2. Stir in the butter and grenadine to make a pale pink sauce.

Makes 1 litre/1 ¾ pts/4 ¼ cups

Index